Basement
stock

LL 60

HISTORIC FULWOOD
AND CADLEY

Historic Fulwood and Cadley

'Where there once was a forest'

CAROLE KNIGHT

&

MARGARET BURSCOUGH

Carnegie Publishing, 1998

07719723

First published in 1998
by Carnegie Publishing Ltd, Chatsworth Road, Lancaster LA1 4SL.

British Library Cataloguing-in-Publication data
A catalogue record for this book is available from the British Library

ISBN 1–85936–044–0 (*hardback*)
ISBN 1–85936–061–0 (*softback*)

Typeset and originated by Carnegie Publishing
Printed and bound by Cambridge University Press

Contents

Introduction

 HERE WAS ONCE A FOREST – a vast wooded area in the north-western corner of England. The most notable landmarks in this territory were the rivers and streams which wound their way from the central uplands, through the flat plains of the Fylde to the coast. Just north of one such river, the Ribble, was a small section of forest which secured for itself a unique identity and, in so doing, a rightful place in history.

Fulwood: marched over by Roman soldiers, occupied by Anglo-Saxon and Scandinavian invaders, appropriated by one parish but coveted by another, and finally, urbanised by nineteenth-

and twentieth-century developers. Research reveals this colourful past, providing material for a fascinating chronicle of a small community and its environment. A radical change in the landscape is only part of the story; perhaps more interesting are the lives of those who, sometimes albeit unlawfully, brought about this transformation.

Fulwood's past has been well documented since the thirteenth century, when the boundaries of this ancient township were firmly established by order of the king. The first part of this book, covering these earlier centuries, is based on original maps and documents and on previously published local history material. A natural division occurs in the nineteenth century when the Moors of Fulwood and Cadley were enclosed by an Act of Parliament. New roads were built and the land granted to the original tenants, or sold to developers. As the story of modern Fulwood and Cadley unfolds, the text is illustrated by a collection of old photographs, recording familiar scenes as they were in a bygone age. The roads and houses of old Fulwood, with their rich legacy of Victorian and Edwardian architecture, are permanent monuments to the history of this fine suburb.

Acknowledgements

N WRITING this comprehensive book of the history of Fulwood and Cadley the authors have been helped by many people in different ways.

For their encouragement and advice they would like to thank Marian Roberts, Leo Warren, Rachel Quine, Jennifer Holden, Judith Boxall, Nigel Morgan, Margaret Powell, Joe Walton and Marion Brogan, also David and James.

Many of the photographs have come from private collections and we are very grateful to the owners for allowing us to reproduce them. In particular we must single out Brian Swarbrick for offering us unrestricted choice from his collection of old postcards.

Much of the material used has been drawn from original documents, photographs, old books and maps held in the archives of the Lancashire Record Office; the Harris Museum and Art Gallery; the Harris Reference Library; the Lancashire Evening Post; Fulwood Barracks Museum; and the Commission for New Towns. We would like to thank all their staff who have kindly given help and advice in locating and supplying relevant sources. Where necessary, permission to reproduce has been obtained and is acknowledged with thanks. To assist other local historians, wherever possible the source of material, location and reference numbers are printed in a Further Reading section at the end of the book. We have made every effort to ensure that all facts are accurate, but apologise if we have unwittingly made any errors.

We would like to thank the staff of Carnegie Publishing Ltd for an excellent production.

On a personal note we would both like to thank our husbands for their forbearance and encouragement during the past year whilst we have been researching and producing this book.

Finally we would like to dedicate this volume to all those

who live in Historic Fulwood and Cadley, and hope that they will have as much pleasure reading it as we have had in writing it.

Carole Knight and Margaret Burscough

CHAPTER ONE

The First Millennium

 HE STORY OF FULWOOD in Lancashire should begin at the Conquest of England by King William of Normandy in 1066. It is due to him and his followers that Fulwood came into existence, was given its purpose and its name, and first acquired documentary records.* There is, however, a much earlier unrecorded history to be told, of a sparse indigenous population living here throughout the eventful years of the first millennium. These people helped to develop the English way of life and contributed much to the character and culture of this district. Over the centuries they were subjected to a succession of invaders and marauders who either conquered their lands and then departed, or overran and colonised them. So that, in 1701, Defoe could describe 'The True-born Englishman' as 'your Roman–Saxon–Danish–Norman English'.

The first outsiders to make their mark on this landscape were soldiers of the Roman army who arrived in the north west of England in AD 79. Julius Agricola conquered all this part of Brigantia and established forts at Wigan, Ribchester, Kirkham and Lancaster with a service station at Walton-le-Dale. A road system connected these forts to the legionary headquarters at Chester and York. Two military roads, built by conscripted local Britons, crossed in the centre of Fulwood. They were the south–north link from Chester to Lancaster which crossed the bridging point of the Mersey, Ribble and Lune estuaries; and the east–west one from York. This route penetrated the Pennines through the Aire Gap and continued via Ribchester to Dalebrig (Dowbridge),

---

* The names 'Fulwood' and 'Lancashire' have been used occasionally in the first section of this book even though they did not exist until the twelfth/thirteenth centuries.

east of Kirkham. The military forts and stations were always built in a straight line and between fifteen and twenty miles apart, the distance that could be covered in a good day's march. So there was no outpost in the Fulwood or Preston area. The importance of the North West to the Romans was purely strategic in providing western military routes from the south to Hadrian's wall and Scotland.

They seem to have had little influence here on the scattered local population of Celtic-speaking Britons. The original islanders kept their own language which we still use in the names for local rivers and settlements – Ribble, Darwen, Hodder, Wyre and Calder; Savick, Tulketh, Inskip, Treales and so on. The routes of the two Roman roads survive in Fulwood today, roughly along Garstang Road and Watling Street Road.

The Romans departed from Britain at the end of the fourth century, and there followed several centuries which have since been labelled The Dark Ages. The lands of the North West were left in peace for 200 years until, once again, at the end of the sixth century invaders came. These marauders were Anglo-Saxons from the Baltic coastlands. Angeln at the southern end of the Danish peninsula was their chief centre and gave them their name, 'Anglians'. They came from the east through the Ribble Valley and along the Roman road. For a while they lived peaceably with the Britons. But in AD 615 their leader Ethelfrith's victory at the Battle of Chester ensured the supremacy of the Anglo-Saxon 'English' and won them Lancashire.

Their influence in these parts, isolated and remote from the kingdom of Northumbria, was, however, a much more gradual process than elsewhere in the country. They made settlements and named them Ashton, Lea, Broughton, Barton, Haighton, Fishwick, Newsham, Walton and Preston. The name Cadley itself dates from this period and is thought to derive from a chieftain named Caedes who owned this land.

In the middle of the seventh century AD when the Northumbrian King Eegfrith sent a Saxon prince to rule over that part of Deria which later became Lancashire, he found British priests here holding land on the banks of the Ribble. A grant of lands on the Ribble was made in 670 to St Wilfrid's abbey at Ripon. To this day Preston's coat of arms bears St Wilfrid's emblem,

Arms of Saxon Kings. The district now known as Fulwood was in Saxon times part of the kingdom of Northumbria. In 549 King Ella established the province of Deira, part of which

ULSHERE,
King of Northumberland,
Anno 659.

EGBERT, King.—Anno 840.
ALFRED, King.—Anno 872.

EDGAR, King.—Anno 956.
ETHELRED, King.—Anno 979.

later became Lancashire. His son Edwin was the first Christian King of Deira from 617, and one of its few rulers to die a natural death.

the Pascal Lamb (Agnus Dei) with the initials P.P. - Prince of Peace (Princeps Pacis). The word Preston, or Priests' town, comes from the name the Anglo-Saxons gave to it 'Presta-Tun'.

At the beginning of the tenth century in AD 902 a large number of new immigrants landed along the coastline of Lancashire. They were Irish Norsemen, fair-haired Fingalls originally from Norway. Over the previous century the Vikings had invaded and terrorised Ireland. But for over twenty years this group had settled along the east coast of Ireland trading and engaging in commerce. It was a quiet period for them as they put down roots in the Dublin area. Some married Irish wives and became Christians. Meanwhile, the Irish clans who had been fighting amongst themselves began to get the upper hand in their resistance to the Norse. In a battle at Dublin 800 were slain, including Olaf their leader. Six years later in 901 the indigenous Leinstermen captured the city and the Norse were driven out. They escaped across the Irish Sea and arrived on the west coast of England and Wales. Many of them crossed the flat plains of the Fylde and arrived in north Preston, bringing their language and culture to the local Anglo-Saxon population. Although the numbers coming grew to a near mass-migration, they were easily absorbed in these largely unoccupied lands of the North West. As land-owners they were encouraged to settle down to farming and developing their settlements. The names Garstang, Grimsargh and Goosnargh are Irish/Norse – 'Gusan', an Irishman, held an 'arg' or pasture there. This Irish/Norse element of their language is unique to the North West, although pure Scandinavian names abound elsewhere.

There were two Norsemen called Ravenkel and Mamegil who owned land in Fulwood. Ravenkel, who held Woodplumpton in thegnage,* had a hey for enclosing wild cattle (at the site of the present Plungington Hotel). Mamegil's plot was at the west of Cadley near to Woodplumpton. One of their chieftains, Agmundr, sometime between 900 and 930, gave his name to Amounderness, his territory which included all the land north of the Ribble and south of Wyresdale. The Fylde coast and the Forest of Bowland formed its east and west boundaries. King

---

* *thegnage*: land held in service to the king.

Athelstan (924–39) gave this land 'to God, St Peter and the church at York'. Amounderness is still the official name of the district in which Fulwood stands.

EDWARD THE CONFESSOR,
King.—Anno 1042.

In the year 1840 an exciting discovery was made which yielded a hoard of treasure from this period. Workmen reinforcing the banks of the River Ribble near Cuerden unearthed a chest which had probably been buried in about AD 905. The lead-lined box contained about 7,000 coins, some of them Irish, and much other treasure, including broken jewellery. Most of the hoard was deposited in the British Museum, but a few coins can be seen in Preston's Harris Museum. The reason for its burial is uncertain. An interesting theory put forward by David Hunt in his *History of Preston* (1992) suggests that the chest may have contained the funds of Norse forces assembling in the Ribble valley for a (frustrated) campaign to win back their settlement in Ireland. Another archaeological find was made early in the same century by John Weld at Claughton-on-Brock. He discovered an earthen burial-cairn dated to about AD 900, which, alongside the human remains of a Viking chieftain and his wife, contained a box of silver jewellery. A 'tortoise' brooch was similar to the ones possibly made in Norse settlements in Ireland. These two 'finds' brought to life an era about which little is known. The local population were a simple peasantry, engaged in subsistence farming, and of interest to their overlords only in terms of the amount of taxes they paid, in the form of 'Danegeld' to bribe the Danes to stay away, and 'firma' demanded by the King. Their peaceful way of life in this land north of the Ribble was, however, to be shattered in a dreadful way.

Amounderness in the 1060s was held by Tostig, son of Earl Godwin of Essex, whose brother Harold became King of England. As a result of Tostig's treachery, which led to the Battle of Stamford Bridge, King Harold's army was badly weakened and lost its next battle against William of Normandy at Hastings. Harold was killed and William seized the Crown and lands of England.

One of Harold's supporters, Germot of York was stirred to take revenge against Tostig who had been killed at Stamford Bridge. He made a marauding foray into Amounderness, overran the countryside, pillaging it and leaving it near derelict. All Tostig's supporters were killed.

King William's Norman Army, faced with rebellion by the northern Earls Edwin and Morcar, completed its devastation, burning the town and villages of Preston. Such was the situation when the Domesday Book was published in 1086. In the area around Preston sixteen settlements had 'few inhabitants'; a large unspecified number were described as 'lying waste'.

A Saxon poet spoke from the heart when he wrote these lines:

> Cold heart and bloody hand
> Now rule the English land.

So ended 1000 years of history, the first millennium, with the lands north of the Ribble in a state of wilderness. The Anglo-Saxons undisputedly left behind them a valuable legacy, an established social and political organisation, and the English language which we speak today.

CHAPTER TWO

The Royal Forest of Fulwood

The Norman Kings and their Royal Forests

Before the Norman conquest of 1066 most of the woodlands of
England were open to everyone, providing all the timber needed
for housebuilding and fuel. Farmers fenced their fields and made
their tools and agricultural machinery with wood. Birch and hazel
were used for stoking forges; willow, bracken, gorse and heather
for thatching, basket-work and heating ovens. A regular supply
of wood was essential in daily life.

The arms of Roger of
Poitou.

The Norman invaders had a long tradition of hunting wild
beasts, and a greater passion for this pastime than earlier Saxon
Kings. King William seized ownership of all the land of England.
He took about one fifth for himself, gave one-quarter to the
Church, and most of the rest to his followers. The Saxon land-
owners soon lost all their lands.

The King then took possession of all forests and woodlands in
England and Wales, enclosing thousands of acres of woods, heath
and moorland to become Royal hunting parks. Local people were
forcibly excluded and deprived of their customary access for
timber, and for fresh meat in winter. Wild boar and cattle, smaller
game, warren animals, hawks and all trees and underwoods, were
protected by new laws against intruders. The taking of wood,
poaching, keeping greyhounds and carrying bows and arrows or
axes, became punishable offences 'against the Royal will'.

Anyone who lived in or near the forests had to mutilate, or
'lawe', their dogs by cutting out three claws from their forefeet
so that they could not be used for hunting.

The forests were policed by hated 'verderers' who held regular
courts called 'eyres'. The most extreme sentences passed were
the blinding and even castrating of offenders, but the most

common ones were incarceration in gaol or fines of varying amounts.

Deer had become sacrosanct as 'Royal' beasts and had to be preserved undisturbed in their natural habitat, whatever the cost.

There could be no moral justification for the action of the monarchs in enclosing the forests merely to use them as private leisure grounds. Their subjects suffered great privations throughout the following centuries.

Fillewood 1199, Fulwode 1228, Foghellwood 1334
The formation of the Royal Forest of Fulwood

The Norman Invasion changed the course of England's history. In Amounderness it led to the establishment of The County of Lancashire and the district of Fulwood. This hitherto unnamed territory at last secured for itself an identity and a place on the map.

The devastated land had to be reorganised and redeveloped. King William granted Amounderness to Roger of Poitou, and he set about forming within it yet another hunting ground for the King: the Royal Forest of Lancaster. Oak and ash trees and undervert were planted, interspersed with glades and land left open for pasture and arable farming. The south-western corner of this forest became known as Fillewood Forest, enclosed within

King John's Arms. King John reigned from 1199 to 1216 and gave rights in the Forest of Fulwood to the townspeople of Preston.

11

its own boundaries. Benedict Gernet bought the serjeancy of the forest for 40 marks, and he and his family at Lancaster Castle had jurisdiction over it for many generations.

Although successive monarchs extended other royal forests and continued to apply the forest laws vigorously, it does seem that Fulwood Forest was a more peaceful place than those in other parts of England, where riots and angry disputations followed heavy enforcement of the laws. The Earls of Lancaster themselves became renowned for their horse and cattle breeding over a long period. Their success prompted the comment that 'there is no such cattel be, for largenesse, horn and haire as these of Lancashire'. Earl Thomas (Plantagenet) was reputed to have had 1500 horses.

When King John came to the throne in 1199 he was prepared to negotiate with the knights living in the forests of the Royal 'Honour' of Lancaster. For the sum of 700 pounds weight of silver collected from them and from the thanes (the wealthier landowners) and free tenants, he granted them the freedom 'to

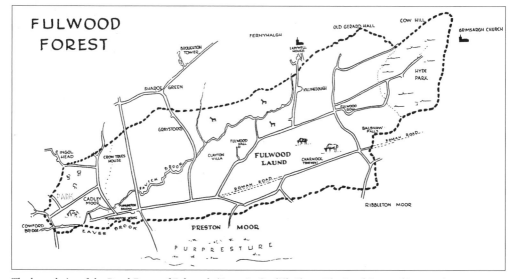

The boundaries of the Royal Forest of Fulwood. (From R. Cunliffe-Shaw, *The Royal Forest of Lancaster*)

The purpresture marked south of Eaves Brook was the earliest part of the forest to be cleared after the Royal Charter of 1199 gave Preston people pasturage and other rights there. Successive monarchs extended this privilege, acknowledging the growth of Preston as an important trading centre.

In 1252 Henry III decreed that this parcel of land, totalling 324 acres, should belong to Preston and not to Fulwood and that the burgesses could cultivate the land and, if necessary, extend their town without the hindrance of the royal forester.

Much of this area now constitutes Moor Park.

cultivate their lands at will, without disturbance of the King's bailiffs'.

The people of Preston also benefited from King John's need to refill the royal coffers. Before he came to the throne his brother King Richard had given him the royal prerogative of the forests of Lancaster. He relaxed some of the forest laws, allowing Preston people pasturage in Fulwood 'for their cattle to be led out at daybreak and driven home at even'. They were also free to take as much windfallen wood for fuel and housebuilding as they required. As in the case of Lancaster, in 1199 for a fee of 500 pounds weight in silver he granted them a charter with valuable rights.

From that date they would be permitted 'to clear and thin and to sell and grant their own woods. Also to hunt and take hares and foxes and all manner of wild animals except deer, cattle, roebuck and wild cattle, in all parts of his forest except in the demesne woods and inclosures.'

Regular inspections of the forest boundaries were made by the King's men. After a perambulation by twelve knights in 1255, they reported that Fulwood Forest covered 2117 acres in the valley of the Savock rivulet, stretching from Cowford Bridge in the west to Grimsargh in the east. The north and south boundaries were the Sharoe and Eaves brooks. In their words: 'Fulwude by the bounds to wit from The Hay of Ravenkel unto the way of Dunpul and thence as the watercourse runs to Dupedale and thence to the upper head of the Lund and thence as the watercourse of Dupedale goes to Fulewude and falls into Uctredesgate and thence as it goes to Lower Coleford and falls down to Cadileisahe'. Ravenkel was a Saxon landholder; Dupedale was Deepdale; Uctred was a King's man whose land formed the boundary near Watling Street Road; Lower Coleford is in the Woodplumpton Road area; and finally came the shaw of Cadeleigh.

The word Savock may have come from the Old English 'sam-ach', meaning 'a quiet stream'. Another possibility is that it derives from the monks whom Count Stephen brought from France to found the monastery at Tulketh in the twelfth century. They were members of the Savigny Order of Cistercians, and later went on to found Furness Abbey. The brook's name was sometimes spelled 'Savig' in early papers.

Despite royal protection the removal of timber from Fulwood accelerated throughout these times, so that by the end of the century the forest had become 'sore destitute of wood', and reverted in part to moorland. Heavy taxes were charged on assarted (cleared) lands, so much of the land was left to go out of cultivation. But at the Eyre of 1334 the verderers complained that the uncultivation was spreading to the greatest part of the forest, and ordered that the land should be sown again with corn.

As inroads were made and the woodlands were cleared, settlers enclosed plots and built houses. This was tolerated on a small scale and fines were duly assessed by the verderers and paid to the crown for the privilege of grazing cattle, sheep and pigs. Even the Vicar of Preston offended by keeping a flock of sheep on the moorland unlawfully. This was not an unusual offence and would bring the vicar a good profit. The English clergy had never accepted the Forest Laws from their first inception, and considered them unlawful. Moreover, they had expected to be exempted from them by the early kings and were furious to be given no special licence. So they treated them with contempt and were constantly in court charged with every offence in the new law books, from hunting deer and keeping greyhounds, to taking timber and undervert.

While there were still plenty of trees in Fulwood in 1373, the Chief Forester was ordered to deliver to the Duke of Lancaster's Chancellor, Mr Ralph de Ergham, four oak trees from the forest complete with bark and branches, to make pales round his Chapel of St Mary Magdaleyne in Preston (at Maudland). At that time the trunks of 15 oak trees were sold for the sum of one pound one shilling and ten pence. It was said that nearly every house in Preston was fenced with blackthorn from the underwoods, bringing the complaint that natural 'cover' for deer was thus being reduced.

The deer, however, were fast disappearing from these parts and with them the Kings' interest in Fulwood. Charles I in 1630, declared that 'the deere there doth now yield unto us little or no benefitt or pleasure in regard the deere, and the woods there have been long since destroyed and spoiled'.

William of Orange was the last king to enquire about the numbers of deer breeding in Fulwood and he was notified that there were none. The old-style forest life was gradually changing, as the whole of Fulwood eventually became moorland, with rough grazing on the higher slopes to the east and arable on the lower level parts.

There was a significant change, too, in the Royal Forest's administrative system and in the nature of the ancient posts of the chief officers. By the end of the seventeenth century these were all vested in one man, Daniel Hoghton, and their value now lay more in their political influence at the County Elections. He sported the titles Bow-bearer, Chief Ranger, Steward, Master Forester, Keeper of the Parks, as well as being Steward of the Manor of Amounderness.

This was a very far cry from the power held by the early officers who held their posts 'in service' to the king.

Fulwood's attachment to Lancaster

At the time of the Norman invasion the old Saxon monasteries needed to be reformed. King William instigated a period of building which produced new monasteries, churches and nunneries in every part of England. Shortly after the conquest, he bestowed land in Lancaster on his kinsman Roger de Poitou. Roger built a castle and church there in 1094 and brought Benedictine monks from the abbey of St Martin at Seés in Normandy, to form the Priory of St Mary in the new church. To provide some income, he gave the Priory the right to the tithes from the Royal Forest of Fulwood, 'for the sustenance of the monks who celebrate the service to God and St Mary in the Monastery of Lancaster.... and none of my successors may have power over these things'. This began Fulwood's long legal attachment to Lancaster.

The parish of St Wilfrid at Preston (now St Johns), whose nine townships surrounded Fulwood, always coveted this gift, and considered the tithes should rightfully be theirs. They made several strong but unsuccessful bids to claim legal entitlement, the last one in 1323. Their failure meant that for the next 600 years the Priory of St Mary continued to collect this lucrative income from Fulwood.

In 1323 both towns were desperate for money. Robert the Bruce had rampaged through them in the previous year, torching their buildings and devastating the land. The foray was said to be in reparation for the 'unspeakable miseries' inflicted on the Scots by the English army at the Battle of Bannockburn. As was often the case, devastation of the land led to poverty and starvation in the local population, lowering their resistance to disease.

In 1349 the 'Black Death', or bubonic plague, which had rampaged through Europe and the south of England spread to Lancashire and was soon raging through Preston and Lancaster. In these two parishes alone over 6000 people died. The figure sounds enormous, but was supplied by a jury and is considered to be correct. More than one million people, over one third of the population, died in England in the three years

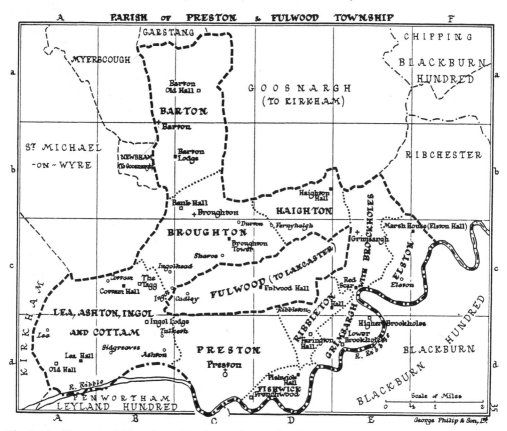

The Parish of Preston and Fulwood township. (From *The Genealogist's Atlas of Lancashire*)

The Forest of Fulwood became part of the parish of Lancaster, completely surrounded by nine townships of the parish of St Wilfrid at Preston. The tithes of the forest were always coveted by Preston, who made several unsuccessful attempts to claim them. Fulwood was finally incorporated into the Borough of Preston in 1974.

King Edward III, 1327–1377. King Edward marched through Fulwood in 1336 on his way to Hallidown Hill in Scotland where he won a great victory. He had halted in Preston for a short break to recruit men for his army. John of Gaunt, his son, married Blanch daughter of Henry, first Duke of Lancaster and became the second Duke of Lancaster. Edward made Lancashire a Palatinate with its own seal.

of this unprecedently severe outbreak. The affliction, labelled the 'forin dethe', affected all levels of society, killing even the great Henry, First Duke of Lancaster, and the vicar of Lancaster. The chapel of St Mary Magdaleyne at Maudland was empty of people for eight weeks at the height of the virulence. A chronicler wrote 'the cattle roamed masterless over the countryside, crops rotted in the fields for lack of hands to reap them and there were not enough priests to bury the dead'.

The consequent great shortage of agricultural labourers to work in the fields led to a huge rise in their wages. By the time the outbreak began to ease off, after about five months, the price of food had risen threefold. Local farmers and landowners were exploiting the situation to recoup their earlier losses. At Preston an inquisition was held to deal with the problem. A great number of charges were made against the offenders under the 'Statute of Labourers Act'. This was a new law recently passed to control and regulate labourers' pay and protect the economy.

The plague lingered on with lesser outbreaks for several decades. In 1390 it reappeared in this district. The people of Preston, in desperation, wrote to ask for assistance from the King, Henry IV, as there were not enough able-bodied men left to defend against the threat of Scottish marauders. A sad postscript to the devastation caused by the 'Black Death' was that the people were convinced they were being 'cursed by the wrath of God for their sinnes'.

Arms of Henry, first Duke of Lancaster, 1356. Henry, son of Edmund Earl of Lancaster was appointed first Duke of Lancaster by Edward III in consideration of his great services to king and country. He kept 40 lancers to guard the sea coasts of Lancashire. In the second outbreak of the Black Death plague Henry became a victim and died in 1361. His son-in-law John of Gaunt succeeded him.

Chancellor's seal of the Duchy of Lancaster. This seal was made expressly for the use of the Duchy of Lancaster in 1416 in the reign of Henry V.

CHAPTER THREE

Cadley: A clearing in the Forest

The Norman settlement at Cadley

The name Cadley is thought to derive from the Anglo-Saxon 'Caeda's legh' meaning land belonging to Caedes. It first appears in print in the twelfth century as 'Cadilegh parkus' at the western edge of the Royal Forest of Fulwood. A section here had been fenced off as pasture for cattle and for growing corn. Outside the park were two newly-formed small settlements called Great and Little Cadilegh, leased by the crown to landowners and sub-let to tenant farmers. At an early but unknown date a waterwheel for grinding corn was built there on the banks of the Savock Brook.

The enclosed park was granted to the Singleton family, Bailiffs of Amounderness. In 1171, Uctred is listed as holder of extensive lands in Broughton and Little Singleton, held in thegnage from Count William of Boulogne, brother of King Harold. Their name is in the thirteenth-century Charter Rolls of King John, so they are the first known, named inhabitants of Fulwood.

Early in the thirteenth century the family was living at the head of the valley of the Whitinsyke which became known as 'Singletons Head'. This name, spelt variously through the following centuries as 'Thyncolheuld', Ingolheved, and so on, eventually settled as 'Ingol Head', a name which we recognise today. From legal documents we can trace this branch of the family down through the centuries beginning in the year 1225 when Uctredsgate was listed as a boundary in the forest perambulation.

In 1246 Richard Singleton appeared in court at Lancaster Assizes. He was 'guarantor of suritie' for Alexander-le-Flemeng who had been in a fight and was charged with exchanging blows with Gilbert Carnewath. Richard did not lose his suritie, for Gilbert was convicted and fined one mark.

At the end of the thirteenth century Thomas Singleton of Ingolhead, and his wife Cecily, shared out 120 acres of their Broughton lands equally between three of their children, Edward, Helen and Joan. Some of the land there was held from a kinsman, Sir William Banastre by the service of 'a rose and one penny' yearly. This fee was simply a gesture, not to be compared with the 'service' expected in previous centuries, when his ancestors were obliged to take up arms and fight in the King's defence if needs be, to justify their land grants. For the rent ('farm') of Cadilegh Parkus Richard paid 53 shillings and 4 pence to Earl Thomas, who had inherited Fulwood Forest and other vast estates from his father Edmund the first Earl of Lancaster. The Earl's account books show that in the fourteenth century the holding of Great Cadley was in the name of Thomas Travers who lived there with his wife Eleanor and son Lawrence. They were entitled to the herbage from the wood and sufficient (turbary) peat for themselves and their tenants.

Their near neighbours in 1346 were Grimbald, the textile merchant, and Adam. These two men, both burgesses of Preston, were renting assarted agricultural land and had pasture rights in the west end of the forest.

The Singletons were still at Ingolhead and, despite their high standing with the Forest wardens, were not exempt from keeping the forest laws. Having a taste for venison they were often accused of taking deer unlawfully. At the court of 1287 Thomas was found guilty of hunting in Lonsdale with his groom Hanne, using Agnes of Kendall's greyhounds, and killing a stag. He was 'handed over to the prison, ransomed at half a mark and found bail'. His cousin at the same court was in trouble for jumping bail, whilst William, and the brothers Nicholas and John were all fined for taking bucks and does in the outer parts of Lancaster Forest.

In the following century three of their tenants at Ingolhead, William Euxton, John Sparrow and Robert Woodfall, all failed 'to have their bodies before the Justices' in Lancaster in 1396 to answer 'divers charges in breaking forest laws'. They managed to elude the Sherriff's men who dolefully reported 'They come not',

'They have not been found'. The head of the family in 1512 was another Thomas whose well-to-do bride Katherine gave up claim to a list of her dower properties in the Ribble valley, with such names as 'Ffrydaybank', 'Rawslattyng', 'Goosebutts', 'Oxhey and Horsehey'. But they were still flouting the forest laws and appeared in court again charged with unlawfully cutting down and carrying away trees and underwood.

In the sixteenth century England's ministers, in response to the possibility of war with Spain, passed statutes to ensure that the country was prepared, with an army of able men properly armed. Each county was detailed to contribute men, horses and weapons. A general muster was held in 1553. Amounderness had to send 300 men, 7 of whom were to come from Fulwood. In 1574, 23 local gentlemen were given a list of horses and weapons they had 'to put in readyness, to have and keep for Her Majestie Queen Elizabeth.' William Singleton was to supply 1 morraine and 1 caliver (a kind of musket).

The grant of land at Ingolhead had passed to the Earl of Derby. When John Singleton died at an early age in 1588, leaving his widow, Ellen, with four young sons under thirteen years, he held the Cadley estate on lease from the Earl for 'a pair of white gloves and one penny'. His young son Thomas became, in time, the father of the last of the Singleton line at Ingolhead, for in 1631, the heir, John, was struck by the plague which was rife in Lancashire. He died and was buried in Preston parish churchyard in July 1631. His wife and two children suffered the same sad fate within a few weeks, wiping out the last of the family. For the first time in over four hundred years, the estate went out of the hands of the Singleton family.

The next owner was Henry Beesley who moved from 'The Hill' in Goosnargh in 1648. His death in 1666, was followed two years later by his heir's, George. Harry, the eldest of his five sons, lived at Ingolhead until his death in 1702, when it passed into the hands of the Walker family who gave their name to Walker Lane. William Walker was an ironfounder who, on his death, left the estate to his eldest son John. In 1750, John died, passing the land to his three sisters, Sarah, Ann and Jane. Sarah married George Boys of Durton, who later bought out his sister-in-laws' shares and gave his name to Boys Lane. The farm then extended over

80 acres and George was assessed for Window Tax on the eleven windows in his house, and for tithes on the house, barn, old and new orchards, croft, garden and land.

The old house was partly demolished and modernised in 1930. It has been renamed 'Kimberley Lodge'. The name 'Ingolhead' remains on the house formed from the farm buildings.

The formation of Cadley village in the sixteenth century

During the reign of Henry VIII (1509–1547) the status quo in the Royal Forest of Fulwood was challenged by certain burgesses of Preston. They had always coveted the vast acres where they had limited rights to pasture their cattle and take timber. Quietly, over a period of about thirty years, a small determined group of them infiltrated the King's land and fenced off plots where they installed their animals and built homes. Gradually a small settlement grew up around the monarch's corn-mill on the north bank of the Savock Brook (now Mill Lane). The development was unlawful and led to several actions in the Duchy Court of Lancaster. Although the lawful leaseholders obtained injunctions against them, the squatters steadfastly refused to leave their settlement. William and Roger Singleton, John Tomlinson, Grace Shakeshaft, William Harrison, Ralph Hatch, John and Reynold Shakeshaft, and others were charged on several occasions with unlawfully encroaching upon and enclosing land, erecting houses, barns and turf-houses and on taking profits and issues arising therefrom. The leaseholders eventually, however, had to accept the situation and set up proper agreements and rents for the occupants. So it was that the hamlet of Cadley was founded, the forerunner of modern Fulwood.

After Elizabeth I came to the throne in 1558, she was notified of the new settlement by the brook at Cadley, which was controlled by her court at Myerscough. In February 1576 she leased to Oliver Wrigan of Sharoe 'divers lands, tenaments, meadows and pastures lying in Little Cadley under the yearly rent of twenty shillings and eight pence and our water-mylne there under the yearly rent of twenty shillings'.

The miller in 1588 was Charles Yestwistle. He was followed in 1598 by a new tenant, Oliver, the son of Ralph Hatch, one of the first Cadley squatters. Unfortunately, Oliver died before his son James was ready to take over as miller. His widow struggled to keep the business going, but neglected to maintain the property. As a result the Chancellor of the Duchy of Lancaster reported to the Queen about the neglect of her corn mill, which was an offence against forest law, and indeed about the poor condition of all her land in Cadley. The settlement had grown up piecemeal and was in a poor state. The boundaries of meadows and pastures around the mill in Little Cadley had become intermingled with those in the adjoining new settlement of Great Cadley. He advised that if improvements and repairs were not made soon there was a possibility that the Queen might lose parts of her inheritance there, and Oliver Wrigan, the grand leaseholder, could lose his right to the rentals. Her Majesty responded quickly by commanding Thos. Gerrard, her man in Lancashire, to commission four loyal subjects to deal with the problems. They duly inspected the mill and questioned the local residents about the disputed boundaries of Cadley. From the replies they were given we can build up the following broadly accurate picture of mediaeval Cadley and its inhabitants.

In 1599 the hamlet extended over 40 acres in the Forest of Fulwood, all still owned by the Monarch. There were also two acres of old chantry lands which had been seized by Henry VIII at the dissolution of Preston's Greyfriars Friary in June 1540 and given then to Sir Thomas Holcroft, Knight. (The exact location of this land is not known but the name Greyfriars lives on in the roads off Boys Lane.)

There were about seventeen households occupied by members of thirteen families, many of them descended from the original settlers. They made a meagre living farming their small plots, grinding corn, breadmaking, cutting turves and so on. They paid rent of about £1 7s. 6d. per acre to the Duchy of Lancaster and tithe to Lancaster Priory. James Hatch and his widowed mother paid 20 shillings rent per annum for the corn mill and 10d. for their cottage. Robert Shakeshaft occupied the old chantry lands owned by William Clayton and William Charnocke.

Three tenaments totalling 32 acres, rented by William Harrison, Henry Birches and Margaret Cowell, were formerly one ancient settlement which adjoined the mill and was known as Little

Cadley. These three families had a coveted right of way through the passage which led to the water mill. The remainder of the land lay in Great Cadley. Ancient tracks across the moors (now Brook St, Black Bull Lane and Cadley Causeway) gave access to the north and the coast.

The hamlet was controlled from Her Majesty's court at Myerscough which collected the rents and appointed two burleymen (bylaw-men) to keep the peace. The main problems were concerned with stray animals or unyoked swine causing damage to fields and gardens. Other complaints were dealt with by the Court Leet at Preston.

None of the old Cadley buildings in the present Mill Lane area survived, having been constructed of mud and willow with thatched roofs. It was not until the end of Elizabeth's reign that increased wealth brought an improvement in cottage building with the use of oak beams and plaster. In fact, the Elizabethans were the first people to benefit in any way from the strict forest laws, in that, because of them, the woodlands had at least been preserved. There was thus sufficient timber available to them for domestic use and for the building of the military defences needed in the Queen's troubled reign.

CADLEY IN 1599

Tenants	Age	Acreage	Rent
Mgt Cowell & son	68	12	16s. 1d.
William Harrison	26	16	21s. 6d.
John Harrison	60	1.5	16d.
James Hatch	32	Water mylne	20s.
Jane Hatch	60	cottage	10d.
Thos. Cornerrowe	60	land	
Robert Wrigan	80	tenement	10s. 3d.
Henry Byrchis	28	4	6d.
Robert Shakeshaft	60	2 (chantry land)	
William Gregson	No details		
Richard Tomlynson	40		
William Arkwright	27		
Robert France	22		
William Watson	30		
Henry Shakeshaft	40		

John Sudell   44
Richard Harrison   66

All sub-let from Oliver Wrigan.

Cadley Mill

Oliver and Jane Hatch came to Cadley Mill in the last decade of the sixteenth century and they and their descendants worked the mill for two hundred years through the reign of ten kings and queens of England. These were turbulent times in which the Hatch family struggled to make their living grinding corn and bread-making. Each succeeding generation lived through devastating events – experiencing civil wars, uprisings, a dreadful plague and the constant penalties and restraints imposed upon them as Roman Catholic recusants.

The first son in each generation was christened Oliver or James and he became the next miller. In the 1590s, the first Oliver paid rent of twenty shillings a year to her Majesty Queen Elizabeth I for the mill, and ten shillings for the cottage. He died in 1599 leaving the mill to his son, James, who was visited by the queen's men and chastised for allowing the mill to fall into disrepair.

By the eighteenth century the family's fortunes must have improved. A will dated 1717 records how Oliver the second divided his accumulated wealth amongst his children. The mill and equipment were left to his first son, James, who was instructed to pay his mother £8 per year. To his second son, Thomas, he left another house called 'Stopforths', and to James, his horses, mares and husbandry gear, as well as his best suit of apparel and all his wool-linens and woollens. The daughters were bequeathed £60 each and his loving wife Margery, all his cows, calfs and household goods. Oliver was a practising Catholic, known to have refused to take the Protestation Oath, and his widow and heir James continued their allegiance to their old faith. On three occasions, in 1715, 1717 and 1720, James registered this fact in the Papist returns, listing the water-corn mill with kiln and turfhouse, messuage, tenement and five acres of land, all leased from Nicholas Wadsworth.

26

A section of the First Edition Ordnance Survey Map, 1849, showing the Cadley and Fulwood areas. Note how many of the ancient names have found their way into modern street names.

James married Mary Eccles of Ingol and their two sons were christened Oliver and James. This Oliver was the last miller named Hatch to work Cadley Mill. He moved to Cark-in-Cartmell, leasing his lands in Cadley to his daughter Ann and son-in-law Christopher Hayhurst. In 1770 he died leaving his lands in Cadley to James, the eldest son. Although the Hatch

This excellent painting shows Cadley Corn Mill, which stood on the banks of Savick Brook for at least 300 years until the 1870s. In Elizabethan times a water-wheel was driven by water from the brook, but the origins of the mill could well be much earlier than that. In the eighteenth century the windmill and the steam-engine mill were built. The brook was dammed, first at the side of the mill and later, again, higher up nearer to the Old Lancaster Lane (Black Bull Lane).

The last working miller was Richard Cartmel, almost 300 years after the first known one, Charles Yestwistle, in 1588, the year of the Spanish Armada.

At the time of this painting William Noblett of Millbank House owned the land and mill properties, and his sister Jane Pearson lived in the little medieval cottage. (*Painting reproduced by kind permission of the owners, Mr and Mrs C. W. Eckersley*)

family continued to farm the land, their long association with the corn mill ended.

Towards the end of the eighteenth century, a new miller, James Knowles of Cadley, bought the land and buildings and worked the mill with his brother John. In 1760 they were listed as owing rent to his Majesty's court for property in Fulwood Forest. Nevertheless, the two brothers worked hard at their business and improved the holding considerably. A windmill was built to replace the old water mill. John died in 1819 leaving estate, now valued at £300, to his widow and five children.

The two sons George and John, who inherited the mill, benefited from the new era of powered machinery, and prospered as none of their predecessors had done. A steam engine was installed to grind the corn and the business thrived.

The Lancaster Railway Act was passed in 1837 and the new line cut straight through the fields of Cadley. Many local farmers were affected and lost parts of their old land-holdings. Hatch Mill was barely 500 yards from the railway which cut the reservoir in two. The Knowles brothers were obliged to sell parcels of land to the Railway company. Three tenanted cottages in its path were demolished. They were continually expanding their business and, in the 1850s, opened premises in Lord Street, Preston, trading as corn merchants. John lived at 'Laurel Bank' and George at 'Mill Bank House'. During George's thirty eight years at the mill, he invested money in real estate and owned a long list of property. He proved to be the last of the Knowles family at Cadley Mill and when he died, aged fifty five, his sons were still minors, so the estate was administered by two neighbours, James Tebay and Richard Boys. The mill property fell into disrepair and a complaint was lodged that 'the wooden bridge near Cadley is in a decayed and delapsed state, and is now broken down and quite impassable to females'.

In 1879 the mill finally closed and was demolished. At the time William Noblett was living at Millbank and farming the land. Mill Bank House was demolished in 1930 but the road names Millbank, Millhaven and Mill Lane now commemorate the historic hamlet and Queen Elizabeth's 'ancient water mylne'.

The Shakeshafts – A Cadley family in Tudor times

Shakeshaft is an interesting name which crops up again and again in the early history of Cadley. One of the earliest settlers was a plucky widow called Grace Shakeshaft who came with the male squatters from Preston to claim a half acre of land on Cadley Moor in the early 1500s. There she built a turf house and headed a family who for almost three centuries contributed much to our picture of everyday life in the hamlet.

There are various legal papers documenting the lives of the Shakeshafts. We know that Grace had a son John, who on his death in 1587 amongst other bequests left 12 ewes and 12 lambs to be shared between his grandchildren. Two of these children, also named John and Grace, were to have 4 ewes and 4 lambs each.

A relative called Robert rented two acres of old chantry lands which had been confiscated by Henry VIII from the Fransiscan Friars of Preston. When he died in 1609 he had accumulated an estate of over £291. His wife Margery was to have their house; his husbandry goods went to a son John; twenty shillings to the children of his daughter Margaret whom she had by William Gregson; and the residue to his other children. This may have been the same Margaret Shakeshaft who died of the plague in 1631 and was buried in Preston parish churchyard.

Three of the family, Robert, Henry and Reynold, all appeared before the jury in Queen Elizabeth's Cadley Inquerry of 1599 and testified about the ownership of various tenaments and a right of way through the land there.

A succession of births and deaths in Preston's church registers reveal the same family christian names, Margaret, Jane, John, Thomas and William, through the seventeenth and into the eighteenth century. Most of them kept to their Roman Catholic religion, some conformed and joined the Church of England. In 1641 we find that John (senior) and his son took the Protestation Oath, but Oliver, on the same list, refused to do so; a family split by their beliefs.

The inventory of goods belonging to Oliver's daughter-in-law, Jane Shakeshaft, at her death in 1719 included two old horses and two cows, two little calves, carts and wheels, saddles, oats hay and barley, brass and pewter, one iron pot and kettle, a clock, and earthenware in the buttery. There were also one swine and trough, a cupboard in the house, a wooden receptacle, chairs and other odd things in the chimney, including coals and linen. All these together were valued at £15 12s. 6d. The clock would be a treasured possession in those days.

To her two daughters, Mary and Ann, she left the bed and other furniture which was upstairs, along with articles in the front room. Her two sons Thomas and William were also beneficiaries and when Thomas died eleven years later his inventory of goods was almost identical to that left by his mother before him, but also included £1, which was the value of the deceased's clothes. His net estate of £41 2s. 0d., however, was reduced to only £7 19s. 1d. after payment of £1 10s. 0d. for his funeral, and repayment of cash which he owed to nine of his neighbours. The clock was, however, still in the house. Neither of the widows who had to deposit these inventories in the Archdeanery at Richmond could write their own names. Each used a fingerprint on wax witnessed by the village schoolmaster John Dewhurst and others.

At least they had a roof over their head, and a means of making a living, unlike James Shakeshaft's family from Fulwood. James and his wife Ellen had taken their four children, Lawrence, William, Mary and Katherine, to look for work in Preston. Their poverty came to the notice of the Overseers of the Poor, and on 29 March they were brought before Richard Addison and W. Bushell. Opinion was considered as to the cost of maintenance of the family. The conclusion was that James and his wife and family should be sent back to Fulwood to their own Overseers, who must receive them, set them on work or otherwise provide for them; for they would become chargeable to the Preston Overseers if they remained there any longer.

The document sending them on their way was signed on Saturday 30 March 1872, 'about 6 o'clock in the evening'. It is not difficult to imagine the plight of this poor couple as they left the town to begin the trudge back to Fulwood with four young children.

In 1762 an order was made by the Justices of the Peace in Preston for the maintenance of an illegitimate boy, the son of George Entwistle, husbandman, of Fulwood, and Margaret

Shakeshaft. He was to pay 8*d.* a week to the Overseers of the Poor for the for this child, and the mother was likewise to pay 4*d.* per week in case she didn't take care of and nurse the child herself. In the following century when census and other official directories were published there were no Shakeshafts left in Fulwood or Cadley.

Cadley School

The first school in Fulwood was built in the early 1700s on land in Cadley where now stands the house called 'Edgehill'. A Preston carpenter, John Hatch, who had associations with the Parish Church, left a bequest of £80 in his will, 'for the maintenance of

Samuel Peploe DD, Vicar of Preston founded Cadley Charity School in 1707.

a school master or school dame for teaching the poor children of Cadley and Sharey (Sharoe) to be taught the principles of the Christian religion according to the catechist of the Church of England, and to be taught to spell and read English'. This bequest was a godsend to Samuel Peploe, Vicar of Preston, who was keen to establish new Church of England schools and churches to counteract 'the scourge of popery in these parts'.

On 7 July 1707 an allotment of ancient enclosed land on Cadley Moor was granted by Preston Corporation to the trustees of the new school. The site was at the top of the hill on the old Preston to Lancaster lane, just northwards of Savock Brook (now Black Bull Lane). A thatched schoolhouse and cottage for the master were built there and the new Cadley School opened to its first pupils. John Dewhurst, who lived with his father at the end of Duck Lane, was the master, and provision had to made for his salary. This proved to be a slight problem to Samuel Peploe, as the original bequest was not sufficient capital to produce the required return. He also had at his disposal the interest on £10, left to the church by a Mrs Smith 'to provide bread for the poor on the day of the sacrament'. He used this and put in another £10 of his own money to make up a trust fund to £100. Three men joined him and invested this sum in a piece of land. Joseph Newsham of Barton, Thomas Whalley, doctor of physick and John Whalley, gent. of Blackburn, on 28 June 1722, purchased from the Vicar of Grimsargh five acres of farmland called High Wood Field and Low Wood at Norshaw Farm, Whittingham. The return from this land was to be paid to the schoolmaster annually. He would give one-fifth back to the Vicar of Preston to be distributed in bread to the poor and as interest on Samuel Peploe's £10. The master received £8 16s. 0d. per annum for his personal salary.

We know little of the early days at Cadley School as no archives have ever been found, but a document dated 1712, concerning such charity schools in Lancashire and Cheshire, states that they were 'for teaching poor children in the knowledge and practise of the Christian religion as professed and taught in the Church of England and for teaching them such other things as most suitable to their condition. The schoolmaster shall attend during the hours appointed from 7 to 11 o'clock in the morning and from 1 to 5 o'clock in the evening in the summer, and two hours less in the winter'.

Besides religion, they were taught reading and spelling, with writing and arithmetic for the boys; the girls learned to read, to knit their stockings and gloves, to mend and sew and sometimes to write. Children were admitted from poor families at the age of seven and not above the age of twelve.

After Rev. Samuel Peploe left Preston, the management of the school was transferred to some local men. In 1757, they appointed James Dewhurst to succeed his father as schoolmaster. He was followed in 1764 by John Sergeant. During these years the school land was increased and gardens and a small orchard were planted. At the enclosure of Fulwood and Cadley Moor in 1815, further land was allocated to the school increasing the holding to about two acres. The plot then extended down the hill to Savock Brook boundary and included a sandpit by the bridge, from which sand was sold by the cartload. In 1825 the school had 25 pupils and the head made his own charges for their lessons.

In 1839, a new master was installed at Cadley School. He was John Townley Alston, then thirty years old and married to Alice. They were parents of three children under three years of age – William, Ellen and James. Within twelve years, another five children, four sons and a daughter, were born at the schoolhouse. Mr Alston taught at Cadley for the next twenty-five years and was the last master of the school at that site.

At the beginning of his headship, the school thrived and an anonymous gentleman wrote in 1864, 'Those who know anything of the neighbourhood know that the school had at one time a considerable local reputation and we are able to judge of its usefulness by the fact that several of our most respectable fellow townsmen received their education within its walls'.

The census of 1851 listed fifty-three children under thirteen years in the village, but it is not known how many were at Cadley School. None were taught free under Mr Alston who set his own rate of fees. In 1847 he was appointed surveyor of the township, which added £17 per annum, paid from the highway rate, to his salary. These items are recorded in the Vestry Book of Fulwood Overseers which also details the problems the school trustees had with their sandpit at Savock Brook bridge. A succession of people

Cadley and Fulwood School c. 1905, taken in the yard at the rear of the old school on Victoria Road is the class of 1905. Cadley School occupied these premises from 1866 to 1938 when a new building was constructed on Black Bull Lane. Christ Church took over the old school in 1938 and it has been used for parish gatherings since that time. (*Reproduced with the kind permission of Mr D.Carwin*)

were accused of taking sand unlawfully, rebuked, and ordered to make restitution of the value. In March 1849, the sand-hole had been closed to all non-residents unless they agreed to pay three pence for every horse load, but there always seemed to be problems there.

Meanwhile, there was worse trouble at the schoolhouse. For several years Mr Alston had taken to drinking alcohol excessively, so that local people began to withdraw their children from his school. It seems that there were no trustees now to manage the school's affairs; so there were no means of removing him. Under these circumstances two inhabitants of Fulwood made an application to the Charity Commissioners to investigate the situation. In an order dated 16 February 1864, new trustees of the charity were appointed and the land and property was vested in the official Trustees of Charity Lands. Mr Alston, realising his position was now untenable, and anticipating proceedings for his removal, resigned his position. He was fifty-four years old and had been master for twenty-five years. It was the end of an era.

In 1865, the new trustees were ordered to close the school and sell the property. The schoolhouse, master's house, croft and gardens brought £550 and the sale brought to an end one hundred and fifty years of education at the first Cadley School. They retained a separate allotment of land the school had owned since the Inclosure of the Moor in 1815. This was on the west side of the lane just beyond Cadley Causeway and was let as pasture. Two months later they purchased Brunswick Chapel on Victoria Road, with two adjoining dwelling houses for £560. Mr Peter Watson gave a donation of £50 which would cover the cost of fitting and furnishing the chapel for a schoolroom. In June 1866, Henry Spencer was appointed schoolmaster of the newly formed Cadley and Fulwood School. Accommodation was provided for him and as payment he received all the fees and part of the endowment. The average cost of tuition was 6d., but this was reduced in special cases and the master was at liberty to charge extra for additional lessons. As well as teaching, he was responsible for keeping the schoolhouse clean and in good repair; this was sometimes a costly obligation, for instance, when a misdirected stone shattered a window.

The former Cadley and Fulwood School building on Victoria Road.

For nearly seventy years, Fulwood and Cadley School remained in the old buildings on Victoria Road and a stone lintel there still bears that name. During this time, many changes to the education system came into operation, the most important being the introduction of compulsory school attendance in 1880. As a result, school rolls increased and bigger and better accommodation was much needed. In 1938 land was purchased at the junction of Cadley Causeway and Black Bull Lane, adjoining the plot which the Trustees had owned since the Inclosure of Cadley Moor in 1811. Here a new modern school was built, just a stone's throw from the site of the little 1707 charity school from which it originated.

CHAPTER FOUR

Manorial Fulwood

The Claytons of Fulwood Hall

When Henry VIII died in 1547 the Crown was passed to his son Edward who was only nine years old. The traumatic years of the old king's reign which had seen the collapse of the established religious order, had left the nation near to bankruptcy and fraught with internal strife. The King, too young to govern in his own right, was advised by his privy council, many of whom had only their own interests at heart. The whole of Edward's reign was dominated by the religious reformation intended to consolidate the Protestant faith throughout the kingdom. It was during this time that a large plot in Fulwood Forest was sold, quite probably to raise funds for the depleted royal coffers. In December 1551, a portion of the forest was granted to Sir Anthony Browne, who, under the reign of Mary Tudor, became Chief Justice of the Common Pleas. The reason why Edward VI granted this sale is not clear, for Sir Anthony was a zealous Catholic who had in the past been responsible for many Protestant arrests. It did not, however, stay in his ownership for long. The land was transferred almost immediately to William Charnock and William Clayton. They set about enclosing their estates but, inevitably, this brought them into conflict with the forest smallholders who claimed a right to their enclosures under the terms of past royal charters. The Duchy Court ruled that Clayton and Charnock should be 'permytted to enjoy their landes', and thus the burgesses of Preston suffered yet another reduction in their common pasture-land.

King Edward VI. Edward was only nine years old when his father Henry VIII died. It was during his short reign that a portion of land in Fulwood Forest was granted to Sir Anthony Browne. It was then sold to William Clayton, who was the first of many generations of Claytons to own the manor of Fulwood.

By the middle ages, the Clayton family were already well established in Lancashire, owning several large estates south of Preston. A member of the family had been named in the Guild

37

Roll of 1542, one of seven who held the office of Alderman, a position of great honour in Guild year.

Thomas, the first Clayton of Fulwood, was the second son of Ralph Clayton of Clayton. He acquired the lands from Sir Anthony Browne by a deed dated February 1552. On his death Thomas left the estate to his first born son, William, who was a Justice of the Peace in Lancashire. Although he is recorded as living in Leyland, William appears to have developed his lands in Fulwood. His will, dated 1631, records the bequest to his wife Elizabeth of 'my land and house and rents in Fulwood'. She died in 1633 and the estate passed to his son Thomas who, during the Civil War, was appointed captain in the Parliamentarian Army under the leadership of Colonel Alexander Rigby. He survived the war years and so did the family estates, unlike many which were sequestrated because of the political or religious convictions of their owners. There is, however, no evidence that Thomas lived in Fulwood; he died in 1669 and is buried with his wife at Leyland. Thomas's eldest son William was heir apparent in his grandfather's will, but it appears that he died without inheriting.

Within the bounds of Claytons' land was the perfect location for a house. In turbulent times, the defence of an estate was a major consideration. The elevated spot chosen for the site of Fulwood Hall availed the family of the best situation the landscape could offer; two brooks, running close-by, even provided the house with a natural moat. The building which now stands on

Fulwood Hall *c.* 1920. Preston Golf Club took over the old hall around the turn of the century and it has since been extended, leaving few of the original features. The seventeenth-century porch, however, has survived and is a lasting reminder of the building's historic past. (*Reproduced with kind permission of Preston Golf Club*)

the site (Preston Golf Clubhouse) was probably not the first Fulwood Hall; this would have been a simple timber-framed building with plaster walls. The date on the later building of 1636 probably commemorates a complete rebuild, in keeping with the fashion of the time. The use of brick was becoming more popular for homes of quality. Its use was a status symbol and in practical terms allowed for the building of a second storey, which transformed the interior design. Old bricks, which are smaller than modern ones, can be seen in the walls of Fulwood Hall. Glass was also becoming more readily available giving rise to the small pane casement window set in a stone mullion. Only one of the original windows has survived and is now in the hallway of Fulwood Hall. One architectural gem which has survived the centuries is the seventeenth-century oak studded door.

In the 1660s the hall was occupied by Robert Clayton, brother of William, who was a merchant. Although he owned property in Liverpool, his residency in Fulwood is confirmed in the Hearth Tax returns of 1666. This was an unpopular tax levied on the number of hearths in the house. The returns, compiled by the local constable, have recorded all the properties in Fulwood, except those of the very poor. Fulwood Hall was the largest house having seven hearths; most of the others had only one or two. William is said to be buried at St Nicholas' Church, Liverpool, but the death of his wife Elianor in 1682 is recorded in the parish register of Broughton.

The estate passed to Robert's third son John who became Dean of Kildare in Ireland in 1708, and on to his son Robert, a Bishop who wrote several theological books. He left the Fulwood estate to his cousin Richard, a member of the Adlington branch of the family. Richard's granddaughter, Henrietta was the first female to inherit and she married in 1803, Lieutenant General Robert Browne of Carrigbyrne. A stained glass window dedicated to Henrietta can be seen in Christ Church on Victoria Road.

Fulwood Hall was sold to James Rothwell in the late nineteenth century and he later divided up the estate and sold it in lots. At the turn of the twentieth century, a new farmhouse (now demolished), was built on a plot adjacent to the old hall, and the ancient home of the Claytons was given a new lease of life by the golf club who adopted it as their clubhouse.

Village Life in Fulwood

What was life like for the villagers of Fulwood nearly 300 years ago? We know that they lived simply by their own labours on their smallholdings and traded at Preston market to supplement their needs. They were totally dependent on the weather. A wet summer would lead to a poor harvest, followed by food shortages, price increases and consequently hunger and even starvation if the winter months were severe. In a good year with plenty of sunshine the people were self-sufficient and could lay down stores to see them through the winter. A new and revolutionary addition to their usual diet was the potato, first grown in Lancashire in the 1670s and, by the 1720s 'plentiful and cheap' hereabouts.

Church Cottage Museum. Broughton. Church Cottage, which dates from the end of the sixteenth century, is situated at the rear of Broughton parish church. It was an inn until 1862, providing hospitality to travellers on the old road to Lancaster. From the eighteenth century onwards the publican also served as a schoolteacher to local children. Although Church Cottage is outside the Fulwood boundary, it provides us with an excellent example of vernacular housing for the period. The left-hand side of the building is a three-bay long-house with cruck trusses; it was later extended with the two-storey addition.

In 1995 the ancient building was restored with funds raised by parents and friends of Broughton School and British Aerospace. It is open to the public every third Sunday of the month, from 2 to 5 p.m.

Rev. Peter Walkden, a diarist who lived in the similar village of Chipping, gives an illustration of life there in his daily jottings of 1725. He says that locals grew their own potatoes, rye and oats. They kept cows, fowl and bees, sold butter and eggs at 4d. per pound and one farthing each, and honey at 6d. per pound. A pig would bring 8 shillings and 6d., and an old cow three pounds and fifteen shillings. Beef was two pence per pound and fresh herrings eleven for two pence. A bushel of apples cost two shillings and coal was five shillings for eight hundredweights (less than half a ton). Most of their trading was done at Preston Market. At the end of the day a pot of ale could be enjoyed for one penny. Rev. Walkden would take his at the Flying Horse Inn. In the alehouses they could play dice or cards, listen or dance to the fiddle and pipe and enjoy a game of bowls. Their children received a basic education at the village school, but most of the adults were illiterate.

The common land of Fulwood Moor was available to the villagers for grazing their cattle. This ancient right, which had survived down the centuries, was of great benefit to those eligible, and regular checks were made to establish the ownership of beasts on the common. Stray animals were taken to the pound or pinfold, which, in its simplest form, was just a fenced field where the animals were retained until the owner paid for their release. While in the custody of the pinner, a charge was made for the animal's keep. The pinfold was usually the responsibility of the manor, and in Fulwood was on land owned by the Claytons at the end of Long Sands Lane. The surrounding field is named on the Tithe Map as Tithe Barn Croft, the location of the old tithe barn. Broughton pinfold, a substantial stone structure, still exists and is on the east side of Garstang Road just before the village.

Roads were barely more than cart-tracks leading from the farms and tenements to Old Lancaster lane. At the top of this lane a spur ran eastwards to the little settlement at Sharoe. The Cow-hill farms were connected to the track/road from Longridge. In the winter all these roads were deep in mud and mire and almost impassable.

The Church Tithe Tax was a great burden to the farmers. It was one tenth of all their income, payable once a year to the vicar of Lancaster Priory. Fishwick, the historian, records that in adjoining Broughton the farmers followed the old custom of 'casting out the tenth sheffe of all their corn and grayn till they had the number ten, and lay them in hattocks to be carried to the tithe-barn'. They were careful 'to savgard the corn from byting and tredding of beasts and from wete'.

Years later in 1839 (after the 1830 law) tithe could be paid in cash at rates agreed by appointed surveyors. Their rates were:

For one cow and calf – half a penny graduating to 6 shillinngs and 8d. for 7 or more.

For a plough – one penny, for every foal fallen 1d., for a swarm of bees 1d.,

wool and lamb two shillings per score, every seventh goose, in kind or 8d. in lieu.

For a mill one shilling, and so on.

From about 1840 the tithes on land were discharged into a single rent charge payable to the vicar. Fulwood and Cadley's ancient attachment to Lancaster Priory meant that although they never had a church or chapel of their own the people had to support a church twenty miles away. They were meant to go to Lancaster for their christenings, marriages and funerals, but Preston and Broughton churches were more convenient in those days of rough roads when mule or horseback were the only means of transport. Moreover most of them were Catholics who, after their nearest chapels, St Marys Preston, Catforth, and Fernyhalgh, were burned down or demolished in the eighteenth century, were reduced to worshipping secretly in their own homes. Their marriages and funerals took place, by law, at the Church of England, but in the 60 years from 1690 only five Fulwood couples were married in Lancaster Priory. Nevertheless all bridegrooms had to pay a 'marriage oblation' to the Vicar of Lancaster. He kept a register of 'Papists married at other churches' and charged them ten shillings for his own dues and one shilling for the Clerks. Some refused at first to pay, but after a visitation by a church-warden summoning them to Court they had to submit and settle the fee. In 1722 it was noted that Lancaster Priory paid the Vicar of Preston 3s. 4d. 'for looking after that part'.

The Sabbath day was observed very strictly and there were rules and regulations about personal behaviour on that day. In

September 1801 a notice was sent to the local authorities, including Fulwood, condemning idle people who played football, quoits, bowls and many other unlawful games. Hunting, drinking in alehouses, swearing, cursing, and non-attendance at Church, were also outlawed. Failure to comply meant penalties of 3s. 4d. for every such offence (the money collected being for the use of the poor). The alternative punishment was that offenders should sit in the stocks for the period of three hours. The authorities were charged to make a diligent and strict search of their district and apprehend such persons and bring them before the justice. Villagers were finally warned to 'Herein fail not at your peril'!

The image of Fulwood people leaping about on the Sabbath, cursing and swearing and drinking etc, belies the picture painted so far of a hardworking close community struggling to earn a living! One sympathises with them at the mercy of such intolerant rules, and hopes they were able to enjoy some hard-earned leisure on a Sunday.

The Catholic Recusants of Fulwood

It is perhaps difficult to accept now, or even believe, that there was a long period of about two hundred and fifty years in the history of Fulwood when certain inhabitants were persecuted and harassed, almost to the limits of human endurance. Some of them were landowners, educated men of wealth and standing; others were simpler folk, such as farmers, corn-millers, butchers and shoemakers. Their crime was that they refused to attend the reformed services in their parish church – for this reason, they became known as 'popish recusants'.

To understand their position we need to look at the historical events which led to this. The Reformation in the sixteenth century had a tremendous effect on the town of Preston and its surrounding districts. The population was traditionally religious, and Catholic, influenced by the clergy and two religious establishments: the Fransiscan Friary near Friargate; and the Hospital of St Mary Magdalen at Maudland. The town had acquired its name Preston from 'Priest's town' in Anglo-saxon times. Such a strong and deep-rooted affiliation to the old religion could not

'Christ on the Cross'. This gilt-bronze figure of Christ (150 × 75mm) was made for a crucifix in the first half of the fourteenth century and would have been venerated locally until defaced or buried possibly at the Reformation. In 1968, it was dug up in a field in Lea. (*Reproduced with the kind permission of Lancashire County Museum.*)

be extinguished, despite the harsh laws enforced against all who remained firmly attached to its practice.

In the whole of Amounderness in 1564 the Bishop of Chester could find not one member of the gentry 'trustworthy enough' to be made a justice. All were sympathetic to the Catholics. Lord Strange described the county as 'so bridled and bad an handful of England'. In 1583, the Bishop denounced Preston people as 'most obstinate and contemptuous of the new laws on religion'. He asked the government 'to deal severely and roundly with these recusants'. For the next two and a half centuries, in varying degrees, they were indeed severely dealt with.

Following an Act of Parliament in 1547, and the Act of Uniformity and Supremacy of 1599, all Catholic chantries and free chapels were confiscated and assigned to the Crown. The Franciscan Friary, already dissolved, was put to secular use and the Hospital of St Mary Magdalen was demolished. Catholic schools were taken over and churches and chapels seized or destroyed. St Wilfrid's Church, Preston, was renamed St Johns and there, and in all local churches, the Mass was replaced by new services according to the Book of Common Prayer. All that was left to the Catholics were their private houses where they would meet in secret to attend Mass and receive the sacraments. They were subjected to regular monthly fines, doubled land tax, imprisonment, seizure of land and even exile and execution. In refusing to acknowledge the Act of Supremacy, they were effectively denied access to universities, the professions and political life, and were forbidden to open schools or to teach. This suppression, however, did not have the expected results. At the Bishop of Chester's visitation in 1605, there were still eighty-seven recusants in the parish of Preston presented at the quarter sessions – some of them described as 'archpapists'.

Over a century later, the religious census registered the number of families in the parishes to the north and east of Preston as two hundred and five Protestants and one hundred and eighty one Catholics. Many of these Catholics lived in the Fulwood and Cadley area and their homes were secretly used as Mass centres.

Families such as the Singletons, who had houses at Ingolhead, Bank Hall, Crow Hall and Broughton Tower, paid their recusancy fines and kept the peace by contributing also towards the Church of England curate's stipend at Broughton Church. When the old house at Ingolhead was pulled down in the 1930s, a priest's hole was discovered on the landing, with another hiding place in the fireplace downstairs where Mass vessels and vestments would have been kept. At Crook Hall, Broughton, in the nineteenth century, a priest's chamber containing a tabernacle, chalice and other sacred objects was revealed. Another Mass-house was William Charnock's home on Fulwood Moor. (Charnock House is commemorated in Charnock Road near Moor Park Avenue.) In 1585, an old priest, Evan Bannister, was brought before the Court Leet and sentenced to be exiled, 'having been caught performing mass here on Lady Day'. The priest was still ministering to his flock in the following year, harboured by Jane Eyves of Fishwick Hall. Ten years later, Lawrence Shorrock, Thomas Lingard and Lawrence Sudall of Fulwood were all deprived of their estates, which were sequestrated and sold 'for treason'. (Under the statutes of 1571 and 1581, it was enacted that 'any person who obtained from the Bishop of Rome anything printed or written, then every act shall be deemed to be high treason, and the offenders on conviction should suffer pain of death, and lose and forfeit all their land, goods and chattels'.)

In 1653 Lawrence Sharrock (Junior) died leaving six poor infants. His administrators successfully appealed to the Commissioners that, as he had left nothing but his tenement, they should release his several closes of land in Fulwood which had been sequestrated ten years earlier, to provide for the destitute children.

Between 1582 and 1680, the period of severest enforcement of Penal Laws, twenty eight Lancashire Catholic priests and three laymen were executed – twelve of them at Lancaster – for their adherence to the faith. Their places were willingly taken by a constant stream of local men secretly educated abroad at seminaries such as Douai College in Flanders which was founded in 1568 by William Allen of Rossall, for this purpose, Valladolid in Spain, and Lisbon. In the first five years of its existence Douai College sent nearly 500 priests back to England.

In 1641–2, on the eve of the Civil War, Parliament ordered that all adult males should take an oath to maintain the Anglican Settlement... 'against all papistry', and also the power of Parliament. Catholics found the wording offensive and refused to take the Oath. In 1641, a list of persons who had not taken Parliament's Protestation Oath included the following Fulwood Catholics: John Barton, Thomas Cottom, Oliver Shakeshaft, Thos. Noblett, Wm. Charnock, Oliver Hatch, Wm. Darwen, Lawrence Lingart, Mr Walmsley, John Savill and Henry Balshaw. After the terrible (and expensive) battles of the Civil Wars of 1642–49 the estates and property of Royalist supporters were seized for Parliament. Large sums of money were extracted from them under threat of prosecution. The Lancashire sequestration committee sat at Preston. Roman Catholics whether professedly Royalist or not were fined.

The aftermath of the failed Jacobite uprising of 1715 again brought great danger and deprivation to the Catholic community. Local men who had joined the Jacobite army and been captured at Preston were tried in Liverpool in January 1716. Twelve of them were executed at Gallows Hill, Preston (now the site of English Martyrs' Church), and four more at Garstang. Joseph Wadsworth was one of those who paid with his life at Garstang. His father, Nicholas of Haighton House, charged with active support of that uprising, had all his lands in Cadley, Fulwood and Haighton seized and sequestrated. The hamlet of Cadley, part of the Wadsworth estate, was predominately Catholic and did not escape unpunished. The corn-miller Oliver Hatch, the Shakeshaft family, the Birketts, Hudsons, Gregsons and Winkleys all registered and were taxed as recusants. John Kendall, shoemaker and tanner of Fulwood and Ribbleton, having been convicted and regularly fined, was seized and confined in Lancaster Gaol. He was father of four sons, all of whom went from the little school at Fernyhalgh to Douai College to study for the priesthood. After ordination they returned home to minister clandestinely in this country. Thomas Cosney of Fulwood registered as a non-juror in 1717, as did the Teebays at Ingol Cottage, Thomas Hatch and John Chew (both butchers), and the Arkwrights, Beesleys and Singletons at the Ingolhead estate. They were all at the mercy of such men as Samuel Peploe, the Vicar of Preston, who defended and helped to enforce the Penal Laws against those holders of estates he considered to be 'granted to superstitious uses'. There are numerous recorded instances of Peploe's pursuit and punishment of Catholics and he was rewarded for his zeal by being made Bishop of Chester. The courage shown by the families who suffered in their determination to keep alive their Catholic faith should not go unrecorded. It was not until the Catholic Relief Act of 1829 that Parliament and the Church of England at last recognised 'the wisdom of mitigating the severity of the Penal Laws' that the recusants could at last come out of hiding and eventually begin to take their rightful place in society. There were more of them in Lancashire than anywhere else in England.

Dame Alice Harrison and her school

Alice Harrison, born towards the end of the seventeenth century at Fulwood Row, was a well-educated daughter of a Church of England family. By reading Catholic books when she was very young, she was attracted to that religion. This angered her father who tried, harshly but unsuccessfully, to dissuade her from becoming a Catholic. She was ultimately turned out of her home. Encouraged by friends and the priest at Fernyhalgh, she set up a private school in Haighton Top farmhouse and barn. This was

Haighton Top farmhouse, where Dame Alice Harrison ran her Catholic school in penal times.

47

to replace the old suppressed school of St Mary of the Well at
Fernyhalgh.

From 1710, for the next fifty years, Dame Alice, at great personal
risk, provided an education for Catholic children. She bravely
contravened the severe Penal Laws which forbade the existence
of such schools. At the same time that the Vicar of Preston,
Samuel Peploe, was hounding the priest at nearby Fernyhalgh,
Alice was developing her little school and soon there were two
hundred pupils attending from all parts of Lancashire and beyond,
at a tuition fee of six shillings per annum.

She was probably saved from persecution by ensuring that her
classes always included local non-catholic pupils. With only one
assistant she turned out a steady stream of well-educated young-
sters, instilling in them a deep loyalty to their faith. A large
number of her boys, afterwards coached secretly by the priest at
Ladyewell, proceeded to seminaries abroad to train for the priesthood, a dangerous career in those troubled times.

In later years they recalled fondly their courageous 'little Dame
Alice' and the local farmers' wives who gave them board and
lodgings for fifteen shillings a quarter. Her little school made an
important contribution to the continued presence of an educated
Catholic community in this part of Lancashire, and particularly
benefited the priests who served them.

Alice Harrison was cared for in her old age by the Gerrard
family of Gerrard Hall, Haighton, and later at their estate near
Windleshaw, St Helens where she lived to a contented old age.
She is buried there.

Sword, pestilence and famine

'In Plague Time' by Thomas Nashe (1567–1601)

> ... Rich men, trust not in wealth,
> Gold cannot buy you health;
> Physic himself must fade,
> All things to end are made
> The plague full swift goes by
> I am sick I must die
> Lord have mercy on us ...

November 1630 was a fateful date in the history of Preston. The Parish Church register in that month recorded 'heare begineth the visitation of Almighty God, the plague'. There had been a terrible outbreak of plague in London and the south of England, which gradually spread throughout the kingdom. All means possible were taken to prevent its progress; travellers were restrained from entering towns and watchmen appointed to prevent their admittance. Trade almost came to a halt due to the fear of infection being carried in merchandise. Public gatherings of any kind including church services were banned, inns were closed and taxes levied to pay for men to apply these restrictions. But eventually, in 1629, the contagion struck in Lancashire, despite all these precautions.

No town in the country appears to have suffered more from its effects than Preston. The Guild Order book records that 'the great sickness of the plague of pestilence wherein the number of eleven hundred persons and upwards died within the town and parish, began about the 10th November 1630, and continued the space of one year. The plague so raged that the town was depopulated, and 'corn rotted upon the ground for want of reapers'. In the first month or two the town's traders refused to accept that the illness was the dreaded plague, for fear of spoiling their market. This may have been the reason for the severity of the contagion and its consequent high mortality rate, for approximately one third of the population died. Even the great plague of London in 1665 did not result in such a high proportion of deaths.

As the plague spread, pest houses were opened and many residents closed their own houses and left to stay in the countryside often carrying the plague to unaffected areas. Judge Alexander Rigby of Goosnargh wrote in July 1630, nine months after the first victims died, 'the sickness in these parts increaseth much and disperseth. It is now in Fulwood, Cadley and Broughton and Kirkham so that the inhabitants and bordering neighbours leave their houses and seek resort to forrein places. I pray God preserve us and stay his hand in good tyme. If it should spread further I purpose, God willing, to send my children into Cheshire'. He had earlier written to his brother in Lancaster 'I am loath to remove rashly because I would not wrong the town by my example'. Although Judge Rigby survived that plague he was unfortunately a victim years later when he and the whole court at Chelmsford Assizes were struck down by a virulent epidemic which resulted in the deaths of all affected.

The authorities in London were informed of the dreadful affliction in Lancashire and instructions were sent by the King 'restrayning travellers and ordering of the people at home for the better prevention of the infection of the plague'. Money was collected from unaffected towns for the stricken people of Preston and district, and at the assizes £60 was granted to relieve their distress. But the poorer people succumbed rapidly. They 'could not long subsiste by their private stores. Their winter's fuelle is whollie unprovided, and all those that live their needes still increase ... all their own helpes being gone'.

An appeal was made to the Justices of the Peace at Blackburn that they might arrange for fuel and victuals to be brought to some convenient place near to Preston's boundary, so that the poor people without carriages could be supplied.

It is thought that the plague was carried by flea-infected black rats which infested towns and thrived in the insanitary conditions of the streets and mud-and-wattle houses. Most of the house floors were made of clay strewn with rushes, under which accumulated an indescribable amount of filth. The rushes would be brushed out and replaced only perhaps twice a year. Even without the plague these poor living conditions could not be healthy. Primitive medicines and treatment probably led to the death of some who with careful nursing might have survived. The illness began with a headache and fever followed by prostration, a great thirst and voice-loss. Within 2 or 3 days sores like boils erupted where the infection had entered the body, and soon delirium would lead to coma then death, often within 6 days of the onset.

Within twelve months of the 'coming of the pestilence' the population of Fulwood and Cadley was decimated. At the time the township was assessed for tax on a total of 51 hearths, which would indicate perhaps 40 to 45 households. From this small community the burials of twenty-five of their members are recorded in the Preston parish church registers, each identified because their place of abode was given. But the numbers were undoubtedly higher than this. The sextons and clergy were under such terrible stress, dealing with huge numbers of burials over a whole year, that they were exhausted and could only scribble long lists of names into their registers, sometimes days after the actual burials.

Names of known Cadley & Fulwood families were entered without 'place of abode', so are not included in the following list. There is a gap at that time in the Broughton Parish Register, but some families would bury their dead in other churchyards, such as St Annes Woodplumpton which held the grave of John Shakeshaft. It is possible that more than a dozen names are missing from the following roll.

ST JOHNS PARISH CHURCH REGISTER PRESTON

Plague victims from the Fulwood Forest community November 1630–November 1631:

Wyddow Shaw and her daughter, de Fullwood
Henry, father of Hy. Sudell, de Cowhill
Lawrence Sudell de Fullwood and his wife
A servant, a daughter, a child of Oliver Hatches
A sonne of Lingarts
A daughter of Jo. Sudells
A daughter of John Helmes of Sharow
Richard Tomlinson of Fullwood
A child of Thos. Ligarts, Fulwood
A daughter of Richard Lingards
A childe of John Helmes of Sharow
John Singleton of Fulwood
A childe of John Singleton of Fullwood
A childe of John Topings of Fullwood
Margrett Shackshaft of Fullwood
John Sharpe de Cadeley

Wm Symson and 4 of his children were buried over a period of just twelve days a fortnight after the plague was supposedly ended.

In the New Year of 1631, as seven weeks had passed since the last death from the sickness, the Court at Preston issued this notice to the townspeople:

Very great care and paines have been taken to cleanse, puryfy and dresse the towne and this Cort thinks that the Faires and Marketts be hereafter sett open and kept.

It would be years before the township of Fulwood could recover from the devastating effects of the 1631 plague. Within twenty years the County of Lancashire was yet again 'in a sad and lamentable condition', devastated by the Civil Wars.

The Civil Wars of 1642–49 turned the County of Lancashire into a battleground, with Preston and Fulwood suffering greatly because of their 'crossroads' position. Royalist and Parliament-arian 'cavaliers' and 'roundheads' fought each other fiercely in the towns and countryside, advancing and retreating up and down the moorland road to Lancaster. Hardly a town or city in the county was not affected, suffering attack, plundering, siege, burning, or killing of the people. Perhaps as many as 1,000 were massacred by Prince Rupert's army at Bolton.

How did this come about and why did Lancashire suffer such trauma? From the beginning the county had fought a losing battle by supporting the King. Only the Manchester, Blackburn and Bolton areas were staunchly Protestant. All of the county's peers, two thirds of the active gentry, and a large number of Lancastrians with Catholic sympathies, were Royalists.

In 1647 when King Charles I was a prisoner of Parliament on the Isle of Wight, he made a secret deal with the Scots that, if they would fight for him and regain him the throne, he would allow Presbyterianism into England. They took up the challenge and mustered their army which, commanded by the Duke of Hamilton, advanced from Carlisle south into England. General Cromwell raced his New Model Army of 9000 crack troops down through Skipton and Clitheroe to meet them. On the morning of 17 August 1648 his advance guard made a surprise attack from the rear on General Langdale's contingent of 4,000 Yorkshire royalists. They were in position on Ribbleton Moor covering the Scots' army's advance over Fulwood and Preston Moor.

The Duke's cavalry, at the front of the long drawn-out line of 15,000 troops, had already reached Wigan. The 5,000 Ulster Scots at the rear were still north of Lancaster. The Duke did not believe that the whole of Cromwell's army was involved in this first attack, and continued marching the infantry southwards, expecting the battle to take place south of Preston. Without either cavalry or infantry the isolated Scots and Langdale's Yorkshiremen put up a spirited defence against the professional soldiers of the New Model Army. Battle raged for four hours, but defeat was inevitable and came by late afternoon.

The Scottish army was cut in two and the northern part retreated in disarray. The wounded and able-bodied survivors tried to escape north and eastwards; the weather was bad and all their supplies lost. Many Lancashire Royalists who had fought with the Scots were chased northwards, and after being pursued for the next two months were finally taken prisoner at Appleby. Bodies of the slain were left on the moorland until men could be found to bury them in a pit on Killinsough farmland in Fulwood.

Meanwhile after fierce fighting Cromwell was able to take the town of Preston, rout the Duke's army at Winwick, and force him to surrender at Uttoxeter a few days later. He claimed later that 1000 Royalists and 500 horses had been killed and 4000 prisoners taken. Ironically the main battle was fought on land in the Royal Forest of Fulwood which only 18 years earlier King Charles had given to the townships of Fulwood and Ribbleton.

At intervals since 1648 relics of the battle have been dug out of the ground. After the enclosure of the moor in 1817, when drains were being laid at Killinsough Farm, 'an immense number' of bones came to the surface. Again, in recent years, workmen building a new road there uncovered human bones. Iron cannon balls have also been found, and at Sion Hill and Gamull Lane lead bullets nearly an inch in diameter have surfaced.

As the Civil War campaign came to an end the County of Lancashire was left in a destitute state. The Vicars of Preston and three other local towns wrote a letter to London in May 1649 begging for assistance and giving this 'true representation of the present sad and lamentable condition of the Co. of Lancaster'.

> The hand of God is evidently seen stretched out upon the county, ... sword, pestilence and famine all at once affecting it. They have borne the heat and burden of the first and second war in an especial manner above other parts of the nation ... The two great bodies of the late Scottish and English armies

passed through, and in their very bowels was that great fighting, bloodshed and breaking. In this county has the plague of pestilence been raging these three years and upwards, occasioned chiefly by the wars. There is a very great scarcity and dearth of all provisions, especially of all sorts of grain ... oats which is full sixfold the price that of late it has been. All trade ... is utterly decayed. It would melt any good heart to see the numerous swarms of begging poor, and the many families that pine away at home, not having faces to beg; very many craving alms ... who were used to give alms at their doors: to see paleness, nay death, appear in the cheeks of the poor, and often to hear of some found dead in their houses or highways for want of bread ... some already at the point of death through famine have fetched in and eaten carrion and other unwholesome food to the destroying of themselves and increasing of infection. And it may be considered that this fatal contagion had its rise evidently from the wounded soldiers of our army left there to cure.

Parliament responded by ordering every church in London and

This unique memorial to the 1648 Civil War battle stands close to the site of the fierce fight between Cromwell's Army and Marmaduke Langdale's Royalist volunteers.

The figures are skilfully carved on the old field gate-posts removed when the approach road to the new junction 31A on the M6 was built in 1996.

Westminster to give half of its collection for the relief of the stricken county. It was at times such as this that people looked for relief to their Parish Overseers of the Poor. Since 1601 Poor Rates had in theory been levelled on all householders in the country to build up parish funds. In times of crisis when all traditional charitable funds had been spent, this money was to be made available to relieve the plight of the genuinely poor. For 150 years the system was not implemented in Fulwood, which was still Duchy of Lancaster land. Its small population consisted of gentlemen farmers leasing land from the gentry, and villages on the assarted lands at Cadley and Cowhill. Their parish was Lancaster Priory twenty miles away, so presumably problems of poverty which could not be settled there were dealt with locally.

As the population grew in the early eighteenth century a group of Fulwood men saw the need for setting up their own Poor Law Relief scheme. Their first recorded meeting was held on 20 January 1751 when a rate of 4 pence per acre of land was assessed on all householders (increased to 6d. and 9d. by 1753). Two men were appointed to serve as overseers for the next twelve months; one for the 'Higher end' at Cowhill and one for 'the Lower end' around Cadley. All local men were called on in turn to serve in this capacity. It was compulsory by law to take on the duties of collecting the 'Poor Rate' and distributing it where needed. Each parish was responsible only for its own registered residents. So 'outsiders' who fell on hard times and could not afford to rent a house worth £10 per annum were obliged to go back to their own parish to claim relief. No newcomers without means of subsistence were allowed to move in, lest they became a burden on the parish. All kinds of problems were dealt with by the Poor Law Overseers of Fulwood. In September 1760 a complaint was made by the churchwardens of the parish of Lancaster about James Rogerson who had moved with his wife and child 'illegally' from Woodplumpton into Fulwood. The Overseers were commanded to remove the family immediately from Fulwood, and to deliver them back into the hands of the churchwardens at Woodplumpton together with the removal order.

In another case in 1802 a single poor woman was sent back to Fulwood from Preston where she had failed to gain legal settlement. The problem of maintaining illegitimate children was also dealt with by the Overseers. In 1795 a Fulwood man, John Yates, was ordered to pay 15*d*. a week for maintenance of 'a bastard female child which he did begat on the body of Elizabeth Anderton of Fulwood'.

In October 1764 the minutes record that the Overseers had 'agreed with Thomas Dickson to go his way for one year with £3 11*s*. 0*d*.'. This was the first of several occasions when this man came before the committee. He seems to have been a vagrant and it was cheaper to give him a lump sum to stay away from Fulwood for one year than to maintain him. Relief payments over the following years were made for a variety of claims, such as for sickness, doctors' bills, surgical appliances, bedding, clogs, hire of looms, loads of coal, straw and thatching, and setting up of apprenticeships with associated 'binding' fees.

Committee meetings were held quarterly at the Withy Trees Inn. In 1816 the owner, James Harrison, was paid 'shot' varying from 12 to 30 shillings for the hire of a room and ale consumed. He was unable to sign his name on the receipt and marked the register with an X. In 1817 Poor Rates were levied for the first time on the land of Fulwood Racecourse and the income from races held there. William Brades paid up arrears for races, plus the Poor rate of £24 14*s*. 2*d*.

The Elizabethan Poor Laws had for over two centuries been administered by local men within their own parishes, although Fulwood's Committee had existed for only 83 years. Populations had increased and the system became unwieldy. Reforms were needed. The Poor Law Amendment Act, passed in 1834, took the Administration out of the hands of these old parish authorities. From that date larger numbers of parishes were grouped together in 'Unions' under Boards organised by London Commissioners.

Fulwood was one of the 27 local townships incorporated into the Preston Union in 1837. Thirty years later the collective problem of Preston's poor was to be resolved with the building of the Union Workhouse in Watling Street Road.

CHAPTER FIVE

Passing through Fulwood

Discovery of the remains of Roman roads through Fulwood

Over the centuries many interesting and exciting finds in connection with the Roman occupation have been made in Lancashire. The discoveries of sections of Roman road during excavations have assisted historians in the difficult task of tracing their route. It was always known locally that there were two Roman roads buried underneath the moorland of Preston and Fulwood, and in 1845 the Rev. John Clay who had seen traces of one of them near to Plungington House (now hotel) and also by the water-lodge of Cadley mill, made enquiries about them. He wrote: 'We were fortunate in meeting a fine old man, upwards of ninety years of age, named Richard Dewhurst, living on Cadley Moor, in a cottage in which he and his father before him were born. His memory respecting this road seemed very clear. He recollected 'hacking up' and carting away seventy years ago the gravel on which it was formed, beginning at the Withy Trees, crossing Cadley Moor, and continuing past Mrs Grimshaw's house in the direction of Cottam Mill. Our informant also well remembered that other road, constructed of similar materials, which crossed Preston Moor and entered the Watling Street. There is enough evidence to confirm that the two roads crossed each other somewhere between The Withy Trees junction and Fulwood Barracks.

During excavations in the 1850s a section of Roman paving was exposed in the vicinity of Lower Bank Road on a housing estate known then as the 'Freehold Park'. The discovery of this road was recorded in the *Preston Chronicle* in May 1861:

A fall of earth by the brookside between Moor Park and

Fulwood Park opposite to Mr Gardener's plot on the latter has disclosed on the Preston side of the brook a very fine portion of Roman pavement being the foundation of the old Roman way from *Coccum* [Walton-le-Dale] to *Bremetonacis* [Lancaster]. It is about two feet six inches below the surface of the soil. The road, which is eight or ten yards wide is formed of boulder stones, gravel and sand and is exceedingly firmly set.

The course of this road had been noted by Dr Kuerden in the middle of the seventeenth century, when he was the Overseer of the Highways. He wrote 'its course was still easily traceable across Fulwood Moor in the direction of Broughton and Garstang, the rampire or raised line of the road was conspicuous'. He also commented that 'The road on Cadley Moor was greater in breadth than the road to Lancaster'.

Clues to the general route of a Roman road are often provided in place or road names. The course of the road from Wigan to Lancaster was marked on a map of 1774 by the names of three fields, 'Great Pathway field', 'Causeway meadow' and 'Pathway meadow', all in the vicinity of Moor Park.

The naming of Watling Street Road in the nineteenth century has left us with a lasting reminder of the Romans' presence in the area and, interestingly, was not the first use of this name in reference to the route. In 1285 there was a mention of 'Wattelinge-strete' in Lea, and again in 1300 of a field there called 'vattelingstrete'. In 1845 Dr Clay twice used the name Watling Street for the old Roman east–west road.

In 1977 an extensive archaeological survey was carried out by John Hallam for the Commission for the New Towns, which involved the excavation of the Roman road to Ribchester at Red Scar. It revealed that this road had been built in two phases. The first was simply a wide clearing edged with two ditches about seventy-five feet apart. This was followed some years later by a road which was flanked by two drainage ditches about twenty-nine feet apart. The surface of this road was laid on a layer of fine red sand and light gravel which was banked up in the centre to provide a camber. Onto this, large and small pebbles were compacted and a line of much larger stones formed the centre of the road. This greatly improved highway was used by Roman

The Roman road to Ribchester at Red Scar. During the archaeological surveys carried out in 1977 by Central New Town Development part of the Roman road to Ribchester was excavated.

regiments as they marched from fort to fort and by wheeled vehicles carrying supplies.

The Roman occupation has held the fascination of generations of antiquarians and their findings have helped in our pursuit of knowledge about these ancient invaders. Who knows what future archaeologists might uncover?

The old roads of Fulwood

The two main roads through Fulwood, Garstang Road and Watling Street Road run south-north and east-west, more or less following the military roads built by the Roman army towards the end of the first century AD. No new major roads were built during the long centuries after the Romans left, and, although the road to the north remained a fairly busy thoroughfare, the east-west road from York gradually fell out of use and almost disappeared hereabouts.

Bridges over rivers and streams, however, even in the wildest parts, were built and maintained under Royal grants called pontagrum. It is in reference to such a grant in 1291 that we first find a mention of the 'Causeway of Fulwood'.

A map drawn about thirty years later, which is now in the Bodleian Library, Oxford, shows Preston and Lancaster joined by a single line, the road which is still used today.

In medieval times when Henry VIII's antiquary, Leland, undertook a tour of England he traversed this road on horseback and wrote: 'A mile without Preston I rode over the Savok, a bigge brooke the wich rising in the hilles a three or four miles off on the right hand, not very far goith into the Ribil were the vast moors and mosses be'.

Throughout the centuries this road was in a dreadful state. Repairs were, in theory, the responsibility of local householders under the supervision of surveyors, but hired labourers often had

Black Bull Lane *c.* 1930. Looking North from Lytham Road up Cadley Brow. In times past, this steep hill caused endless problems for travellers through Fulwood. During the winter months heavy-wheeled wagons and coaches could not grip the surface and struggled to reach the top. Gaskell's grocers shop is now a Spar shop.

BLACK BULL LANE   FULWOOD.

to be employed and a levy imposed to pay for them. This unpopular system was unsatisfactory and difficult to enforce, but it was only in 1888 that local authorities finally took over responsibility for the upkeep of main roads.

Charges of neglecting to maintain the highways were regularly made at Preston Court Leet hearings, and surveyors and supervisors would be threatened with fines if repairs were not completed before a fixed date. In 1670, the mayor, Richard Hind, directed the supervisors 'to pave the causey on the moor leading towards Lancaster' ordered the balives to 'cause a footbridge to be laid over ye brook betwixt Preston Moor and Ffullwood in ye highway leading towards Sharowe and Broughton' and to repair the 'cawseye rampire between more brow and the horse-bridge leading to Caddily'.

In 1675 in O'Gilby's Britannia map the road north was named as a 'direct road' on the route from London to Carlisle. It would, however, be little more than a causeway about two feet broad paved with round pebbles. At intervals there were guard-posts to keep off the heavy carts which were driven alongside the roads. In wet weather the ground often became a deeply rutted mire, so covered in mud that it was often impassable in winter, and baked hard in summer.

For many centuries, the ancient route through Cadley, which we now know as Lytham Road and Black Bull Lane, was the main thoroughfare from Preston to Lancaster. It was described as 'a bad wretched road, in parts not more than a narrow tortuous track which ran through ground covered in rough sand hillocks, meadows, pastures and moory ground'. The people who lived along its route resented having to pay for its maintenance and so it was neglected.

As traffic increased with the coming of four-wheeled vehicles, some relief came to the householders with the passing of the Turnpike Acts, after which local parish trusts were set up and given the authority to charge travellers a fee for using the road. This income was used to pay for better maintenance; so, in about 1755, toll-booths were established at Withy Trees corner and at the top of Cadley between Whittle's cottages and the Black Bull Inn. Charges would be about one farthing per head of cattle and sixpence for a carriage horse. Most local traffic, farm carts and suchlike, travelled free. The toll-bar was similar to a pike and gave its name to the new Turnpike Tax, which in Cadley was collected by the schoolmaster's son, William Alston.

Turnpiking did bring about some improvement, but Fulwood's ancient roads were in very poor condition. They needed to be completely rebuilt to cope with the increasing traffic of the new nineteenth century. Opportunity came in 1811 with the passing of the Act for the Enclosure of Fulwood and Cadley Moors. The Enclosure Commissioners were empowered to rebuild and re-route roads across the newly enclosed lands and to build new ones or close old ones as needed. They decided that the old road north would be upgraded into a new public carriage-way as would the trackway across Cadley Moor (now Black Bull Lane, Lytham Road, and Cadley Causeway). The old path to Ingolhead (now Boys Lane and Walker Lane) would be set out as a thirty foot public bridle-way and private carriage-way. Similar improvements were made to the roads on the eastern side of Fulwood with the building of Duchy Road, Longsands Lane and, later, Watling Street Road.

Jonathan Teal of Leeds and William Miller, land surveyors, were appointed to supervise the work. Contracts were awarded

The bridge over the Savock Brook on Garstang Road c. 1917. Work on the road connecting Withy Trees to Broughton was started about 1825. Bridging the Savock Brook was a major engineering feat because the valley was quite deep, but once completed the new road greatly improved the journey north.

Cadley near Preston.

Looking south from the Withy Trees down Garstang Road. The houses on the left form Park Terrace, part of the Freehold Park estate built in the second half of the nineteenth century.

to Mr George Dawson and others who would level the ground and cover the surface with sand and gravel. The final paving and completion of the roads was undertaken by James Birchall of Wigan and Evan Ratcliffe of Walton-le-Dale.

All this road-building in the year 1815–16 was beneficial to local people and travellers alike. But an even more momentous plan was being discussed by the authorities which would, within the next twenty years, change the local environment forever, and bring a new Fulwood into being. Negotiations were underway for a completely new main road north to be built, cutting directly through the fields and pasturelands of Fulwood Moor.

In 1817 Preston had rebuilt the first part of Garstang Road as far as their old boundary at Eaves Brook. From there the old road then turned westwards past The Withy Trees and Plungington Hotel, then northwards to the Black Bull Inn, and on to Broughton. The new road would connect Preston to Broughton, Garstang and Lancaster in one continuous direct line, and building would begin about 1825. Toll bars were erected at both ends, near to the Black Bull Inn and across from the Withy Trees Inn. Operaters of the latter had the use a keeper's house provided and remained operational for about forty years. (In 1875 the house was demolished and the site was used for the new Fulwood Urban District Council Offices.)

63

One old road which disappeared under the new rebuilding plans was a short 'homestead' track known as Barton's Road, which led north from The Withy Trees area up to the little group of weavers' cottages at Windy Nook. This was lost forever under the new main road. Many of the old moorland roads followed such pathways leading to old settlements, often following the contours of farm buildings and fields. Over the centuries they developed into winding lanes with which we are now familiar – Sharoe Green Lane, Walker Lane, Midgery Lane and so on.

The new Garstang Road proved a godsend to the residents of the Old Lancaster Turnpike lane (now Black Bull Lane) which was thereby relieved of all the north-bound traffic. The ancient highway had done good service, and witnessed many centuries of passing history. It had been fed by the old pack-roads which wound their way from the Friargate area of Preston, over the moor and converged on it near the Plungington Hotel. They too would disappear under the relentless tide of modernisation.

In 1681 the mayor of Preston had offered 'a competent sum towards ye repair of ye way leading to ye west moor', which even then were 'all in great decay and out of repaire'.

Three old Fulwood Inns

'There is nothing which has yet been contrived by man, by which so much happiness is produced as by a good tavern or inn.' (Samuel Johnson's *Life of Boswell*, March 1776.)

The Black Bull Inn

The present Black Bull Inn on Garstang Road is a large, twentieth century, brick building surrounded by a tarmac car park. There is no hint of the fact that this is the third pub of that name to be to exist in the area over the last three centuries.

When William Yates made his map of Lancashire in 1768 the first Black Bull Inn was already in existence, but standing a little way down the Old Lancaster Lane (now renamed Black Bull Lane). It was one of just a few properties on that part of Fulwood Moor, numbering not more that six or seven farmhouses in total.

The old Black Bull Hotel, Garstang Road. 1915. The first Black Bull pub stood some distance down the lane, but when the new Garstang Road was constructed around 1840, this replacement was built at the junction with the new road. The road north narrows to a lane soon after the pub, continuing on to Broughton.

The licensee farmed the fields around the inn, rented from his landlords, Nicholas Grimshaw and Richard Palmer, two prominent Preston lawyers. (Palmer's own parents were publicans in Preston.)

The customers would have been primarily from passing stage-coaches, and travellers on the road north, with local patrons coming from the small communities at Sharoe and Cadley. In 1798 the landlord was Roger Tuson, who held the licence for the next forty years, and paid tithes to the Vicar of Broughton for his crops of oats, wheat and beans. His son James was a teacher at the parish school, and also landlord of the nearby Church Inn.

After the new Garstang Road was built about 1825–30, Richard Palmer demolished the old inn and had a second one built further up the lane at the junction. This was a fine structure, purpose-built to cater for the increasing traffic of travellers and stage-coaches. Stables were provided in the yard at the back and a blacksmith and wheelwright had a forge and workshop next door. The inn was surrounded by gardens, orchards and fields extending over thirty-seven acres. The land where the Black Bull car park now stands was a full-size bowling green.

Roger Tuson retired soon after the move and the new licensee, Robert Wade took over. Richard Palmer, the owner, who had been Town Clerk and Coroner of Preston for the previous fifty years, died in 1852. Three years later his heirs sold the inn and all his lands thereabouts. One hundred and fifty years have passed since then, with a succession of licensees providing just as welcome a pint of ale as did Roger Tuson, and others before him.

Plungington House Hotel

At the Enclosure of Cadley Moor in 1811–15 a large parcel of about 40 acres of farmland was sold to John Myers. Some of the land was on the north bank of Savock Brook, with the rest on the south (stretching the distance from the present Mill Lane to Houldsworth Road). Its eastern boundary met the land of Withy Trees Farm.

There were three cottages and two houses (Plungington House and Plungington Farm) on Mr Myers' allotment and all five had been there when William Yates recorded the area on his map of 1786. To the north was farmland with a single farmhouse by Savock Bridge, and at the top of Cadley Brow stood the old charity school. This was the view to be seen from the gardens of

Modern photograph of the Plungington Hotel.

Plungington House and the farmhouse next door. South of them, open moorland stretched back as far as Preston. Eaves Brook, which formed the town's boundary, flowed through the field behind the house, towards its confluence with the Savock nearby.

Up to 1848 Plungington House was occupied by Charles Birkett.* John Ingham, the tenant-farmer, lived in the farmhouse with his wife Nancy, and a thirteen-year-old granddaughter of the same name who was a weaver. Their servant, Hannah Wilkinson, and a farm labourer with wife and twin daughters, lived with them. By 1851 Charles Birkett had left, and the Macbeth family – Thomas, a tailor, and Elizabeth – were living at Plungington House with their five young children. The three tenanted cottages surrounded by gardens had stood together in a meadow to the south west, but were demolished in 1840 to make way for the Preston to Lancaster railway line.

It is in the 1871 census that mention is first made of Plungington House becoming an inn. The thirty-one acres of pastureland were being farmed by a father and son, Richard and Henry Sutton. Henry lived in the farmhouse, and at Plungington House Richard, aged 70, was described as 'Farmer and Innkeeper'. Although this area was still very much rural farmlands and fields, the house stood on the bend of the busy main highway, the old Lancaster Turnpike Lane. Behind it the old moorland track was being developed as Brook Street, with the new cattle market, and there were cotton mills south of Blackpool Road. So industrialisation was moving northwards from Preston, bringing customers for the new inn. Stables were available at the back of the house for the horses and carriages and carts. In the winter it must have been a dark spot for it was not until 1886 that a gas lamp was put in place outside Plungington House. It was lit only between September and the end of March and extinguished at midnight. On moonlit nights the lamp was not to be used unless absolutely necessary and then only after a long list of rules, concerning the height of the moon over the horizon, had been consulted. The road facing the house (now Lytham Road) was at the time called

---

* Charles Birkett was a descendant of the Birches family who held four acres of land called 'Mowbank' from Edward Singleton in 1598. The land was on the north bank of the Savock brook opposite the Plungington Hotel, where the Derby School was built.

Watling Street Road West; Plungington Road was laid out by 1890 and took its name from the inn. Eaves Brook, which ran through the field behind Plungington House, was culverted and its wooden bridge on the first unfenced road demolished. (*The Happy Haddock* and *Hair Indoors* now occupy the site.)

Over the next fifty years all the surrounding farmland was built upon to form Lytham Road, Black Bull Lane and Plungington Road. Now, at the end of the twentieth century, the Plungington Hotel with its bowling green at the rear still stands proudly on the corner, the friendly 'local' known by everyone as 'The Plungy'.

The Withy Trees Inn

This inn began life as the farmhouse of Willow Trees Farm. William Yates' map of 1786 shows the farm on the west side of the old road north, its land stretching westwards to the boundary of Plungington Farm's fields.

It was first described as an inn in April 1808 when an advert appeared in the *Preston Journal* offering to let the inn by ticket for yearly periods. It was described as 'that well-accustomed

Withy Trees Pub *c.* 1914. There has certainly been a hostelry on this site for a least two hundred years. Originally the landlord would have farmed the surrounding land as well as offering accommodation and refreshment to travellers. 'Withies' is the name given to bunches of willow branches collected for basket making. It was cultivated on damp low-lying land such as the valley of the Savock Brook.

Facing north from the Withy Trees, 1916. The policeman is having a rest from his traffic duties to chat to a group of smartly dressed gentlemen.

inn called The Withy Trees, situated near Fulwood Moor Race-ground, with the stables etc, and about 3½ acres of good meadowland thereto belonging (at present in the occupation of Peter Wearden)'.

In 1816 the landlord was James Harrison, assisted by his father William. They played host to the Fulwood Overseers of the poor at their quarterly meetings, and were paid 'shot' ranging from 12 to 30 shillings for rent of the room and ale consumed.

The name of the inn varied early in that century and was called 'Willows' and 'Within' before it eventually aquired the name The Withy Trees. At one stage, for a brief period, the owner Richard Pedder called it The Pedders Arms.

By 1830 the old moorlands to the north had been enclosed and sold off. With the building of Garstang Road and Watling Street Road, a new era of urbanisation began.

When the Freehold Land Society enabled the Fulwood Park Estate to be built on the Victoria Road/Watling Street Road site in the 1850s, no building was allowed for the sale of beer or spirits, so The Withy Trees Inn opposite became the 'local'. There would have been plenty of passing trade, too, from vehicles and horsemen halted outside to pay their dues at the turnpike.

So, for the next two centuries, with its bowling green at the

back, 'The Withy' plied its trade and developed into the busy and popular inn which it is today.

The Black Bull Inn.

The canal and railway

As the eighteenth century drew to a close new methods of transport were being introduced which would affect the rural landscape of Fulwood forever. At the western edge of the township the famous engineer John Rennie was surveying the ground for a canal which in 1797 would connect Preston to Tewitfield near Burton via Lancaster. When completed, this water highway brought coal from the south and gravel and limestone from the north, to industrial Preston. Packet boats took mail and travellers up and down the canal at a speed of ten miles an hour. During the Preston Guild of 1822 this was a useful means of travelling directly into the centre of Preston and extra boats operated for the occasion. The *Water Witch* was a popular packet which left Kendal at 6 a.m. each day, landed at Preston Wharf at 1pm and eventually sailed back to Kendal by 8. 45pm the same evening.

Although the canal only touched the edge of Fulwood, the effect on the neighbourhood must have been considerable. One benefit was that it reduced the volume of heavy goods being transported by road. These loads were particularly damaging to the road surface and, as the cost of repairs still fell on the local householders, this must have been a relief. Farmers could use the canal to transport their surplus produce to market. Access to the canal from the surrounding farms was probably along the old pack-road which crossed the higher ground of Cadley Moor, the route now followed by Cadley Causeway.

The section between Preston and Tewitfield is the longest stretch of canal without a lock in the country, 41½ miles in total. It does, however, have numerous bridges and at the eastern end of Fulwood there is an aqueduct where it crosses the Savick Brook.

Next came the Preston to Lancaster Railway, built after the passing of an 1837 Act of Parliament, and opened in 1840. This early system was a very primitive experimental affair with small engines which needed the occasional push, and cramped little carriages, some windowless and fully closed, others open to the sky like cattle trucks. The lines were thin and made of iron, laid on heavy square blocks of limestone. This base proved too hard and was soon replaced by creosoted wooden sleepers (the blocks of limestone were re-used in the 1850s in the building of the lower part of St Walburge's Church tower). Although the trains must have looked quite jaunty with their yellow painted carriages puffing clouds of steam as they charged through the countryside, they were extremely uncomfortable for the passengers.

The railway line ran north over Preston Moor and directly through the fields of Cadley cutting the district in two. Some local farmers were affected and lost parts of their land. Near Plungington House three tenanted cottages had to be demolished, the corn mill's water lodge was cut in two and the mill buildings were left barely 150 yards from the line. George Knowles, the miller, lost fields on both sides of Cadley Causeway, for which he was paid compensation. At first it was proposed to build a small railway station at Seymour Road (now Lytham Road) next to the humpbacked bridge. But this plan was abandoned and the site at Oxheys was chosen instead to serve the cattle market.

These last two transport systems had the undesired effect of forming a barrier at the western edge of Fulwood township. The canal and railway line could only be crossed where there were bridges, and these were often narrow with low underpasses, built for the horse-drawn traffic of their time. So access became a problem which still exists in places today. The Lytham Road bridge. particularly, which is too low for high vehicles, has often been damaged when the forgetful drivers of buses and vans have become stuck under it!

Whereas the railway once crossed empty fields and sleepy pasture it now dissects the very busy community of Cadley. The modern, high-powered electrified lines run through the grounds of three schools built alongside it, and there are houses right along its length.

CHAPTER SIX

The Enclosure of Fulwood and Cadley Moors

Fulwood before and after the Enclosure Act of 1811

> Inclosure, thou'rt a curse upon the land,
> And tasteless was the wretch who thy existence
> plann'd
>
> John Clare

William Yates of Liverpool, a surveyor in the Customs and Excise Department, produced a detailed map of Lancashire in 1786. It was significant in that it recorded the county of Lancashire just before the Industrial and Agrarian Revolutions affected and changed its landscape for ever.

Fulwood Moor was at that time still in a medieval time warp. Its population of four hundred people came from 75 families of whom 27 were employed in agriculture, 43 in trade, manufacture and hand crafts, and 5 in other occupations. They paid one penny in the pound to the County Rate of £10 16s. 9d., and lived on land rented from the gentry. The Crown still owned a large portion of the land and the rest was held on lease by the Earl of Derby or belonged to the Clayton family of Fulwood Hall. The land to the north and east of the boundary was dominated by two estates, the Rawsthornes at Broughton Tower and the Gerards at Haighton House.

These wealthy landowners, eager to realise the best income from their land, had put their estates in the hands of gentlemen farmers who managed their farms on a business-like scale. They could afford to build better-equipped farms to replace dilapidated barns and cottages. Yate's map showed these new farmhouses, standing proudly in their landscape. Old estates like Fulwood

A section from Yates' map of Lancashire, 1786, showing the area north of Preston, including Cadley and Fulwood. Note Durton (without the apostrophe!); the windmill at Cadley; Fulwood Row; and Clock House. Note, too, the extensive moorlands around the area, many parts of which still remain as open land, for example at Moor Park, Ribbleton and near the Lancaster Canal at Cadley.

Hall were turned over completely to farming, and extensive outbuildings were built around the old manor house.

There was an old settlement at the eastern end comprising a single line of cottages called Fulwood Row, owned by the Gerards. The tenants enjoyed easy access to the higher slopes of the common for grazing their sheep and cattle. The farthest reaches there were known as Cow Hill. The old tithe barn and pinfold were situated on Fulwood Row.

A small cluster of cottages in the vicinity of Tower Lane was called Sharoe Green, the name meaning 'a spur of land forming a boundary', in this case between Fulwood and Broughton. At the western end was the medieval settlement of Cadley centred round the cornmill and straggling along the route of the Old Lancaster Turnpike Road.

Yates' 1786 map was the first to be accurately drawn and gives a clear, detailed picture of Fulwood and its surrounding districts. The road system shown had developed unplanned from well-worn tracks leading from the only main through-road to scattered hamlets and homesteads.

At this time the poorer local farmers were farming in the same old ways as their forbears had done, merely producing enough to subsist and with no inclination to change. Corn was their main crop, grown to obtain the government bounty, and because there had always been a cornmill nearby.

Cattle which roamed in mixed herds on the open communal moorlands were undernourished, and improvement of stock by selective breeding was unheard of. Sheep were more like goats, bred chiefly to meet the demand for wool. Farming families supplemented their income by spinning, and sold their yarn to local handloom weavers, who then took the finished cloth to Preston market.

At the bottom of the ladder were the agricultural labourers who eked out a precarious living cultivating small allotments and using their rights to the open moor. They too were resistant to change, despite their poverty. When in 1630 Charles I had authorised settlement of some of the moors of Fulwood and Cadley on to the resident occupiers and to the local townships they came secretly 'after daylightgate' and tore down the enclosing fences to reclaim their 'common' land.

After so many centuries of stagnation, however, change was inevitable, and the nineteenth century would herald the start of rapid and irreversible transformation.

In 1793 a national group of agricultural reform enthusiasts came together to form the Board of Agriculture. Their aim was to publicise and popularise the modernisation of farming. They pushed for the introduction of new farm machinery such as wheeled ploughs and threshing machines, and for new methods of draining land, use of fertilisers, crop rotation, and selective breeding. These ideas were taken up by some of the local land-owners and implemented on their estates. Lawrence Rawsthorne of Broughton Tower even wrote his own book explaining the new theories and recommending them to his readers. At the same time they were campaigning for the passing of 'Enclosure of Land' Acts which, it was hoped, would lead to more efficient use of the land. All these innovations, however, would unfortunately squeeze out many of the agricultural labourers. Fewer would be needed in the economy of the new agricultural schemes.

Between 1790 and 1810 over two million acres of land in England, never before cultivated, were enclosed under the new Acts and brought into cultivation. In 1811 came Fulwood's turn. On 8 June a notice appeared, pinned to the doors of the parish churches at Broughton and Preston, and at some local inns, informing the people that an Act had been passed by Parliament authorising the Enclosure of Fulwood and Cadley Moors. Certain tracts or parcels of common and waste grounds totalling 960 acres in the Forest of Fulwood, all owned by the King as Duke of Lancaster, were to be enclosed. Public meetings would be held at the Bull Inn in Preston to explain the situation and collect any claims to ownership of the land involved. The Act allowed that anyone who had made an encroachment on the land already, and had enjoyed possession for over twenty years, would have ownership vested in them. The Act also defined that all previous ancient rights to use of the common land would be extinguished and suspended for ever. After enclosure no sheep or lambs would be allowed on the land for the following seven years.

One twelfth of the moor would become the exclusive property of the King as Duke of Lancaster. Edward Lord Stanley would have the right and interest of this particular allotment for the

Longsands Lane. 1984. For hundreds of years the fields in the area of Longsands were used by Fulwood settlers to graze their sheep and cows. The old tithe barn and pinfold were sited where this lane met Fulwood Row. At the time of enclosure a new road was created which cut through the commonland and divided it up into allotments. The enclosure map names it Fulwood Hall Road but it later became known as Longsands Lane. Traces of the old lane are still evident running alongside the new road.

remaining 27 unexpired years of his lease. No roads must cross this piece of land, but for a boundary on the south side to be used as a public highway. (This last grant refers to the land now occupied by Fulwood Barracks. It was then Lord Derby's race-course.) The remainder of the moors were to be enclosed and fenced as the commissioners judged to be proportionate to compensate those with a just right to the land.

Jonathan Teal of Leeds, and William Miller of Preston, Land Surveyors, were appointed Commissioners for the setting out, division and allotment of the land. Their work was to be done honestly and without favour or prejudice to anyone. Appeals against allotments by aggrieved persons would be heard at the Quarter Sessions before an independent umpire.

There were some other interesting releases which harked back to ancient royal impositions. Immediately after the Commissioners had made their awards, all the lands involved would be exonerated from Game of Deer, Warrens of Conies, and all original forestial rights whatsoever, which His Majesty and his successors might otherwise have been entitled to claim.

In effect the Royal Forest of Fulwood, after 800 years, was returned, freed of royal restraints, to the people. The word 'Forest' was by now a misnomer. Most of its timber had long since been used up for building houses, bridges and ships down through the centuries.

Accordingly, over the following two years all the moorland of Fulwood was divided up into individual plots and assigned legally to new owners. Claims were made by tenants occupying encroached land, and in most cases they received their allotments. Occasionally a challenge was made by a local landowner in the hope that he might overrule a decision, but the smallholders' claims were usually upheld.

At the end of 1813 the remaining land was advertised and sold, sometimes in quite large plots. The purchasers were entrepreneurs of their day who saw the opportunity for future development. Some of them, like the Pedder family and the Stanleys, were already large landholders adding to their stock. Others were successful businessmen from Preston. The millowner Samuel Horrocks purchased 45 acres north of the Preston boundary of Eaves Brook, on the east side of Garstang Road.

Unfortunately, as had been forewarned, those who had never had even a small plot of their own, gained nothing from the Enclosure Acts. They also lost their access to the common land, which had always been available to them for grazing and pasture; so for some this became a time of great distress. Their only hope was to leave the countryside and try to earn a living elsewhere, possibly in the cotton mills of Preston.

In general, building of new farmhouses after enclosure was slow, probably due to the fact that the whole procedure was costly. The first major expense was the fencing of allotments which had to take place within twelve months and required the planting of hedges. Hawthorn, the most common hedgerow tree, was used from Saxon times to form fences to deter intruders and gets its name from the Old English word *haga*, 'a hedge', or 'an enclosure'. Today, the mature hawthorn trees are a familiar sight both in the countryside and in our gardens, marking the boundaries of old enclosure plots.

The Enclosure Award and map is a fascinating document, useful for monitoring subsequent developments. Newly-formed

Fernyhalgh Lane. *c.* 1950. This old lane leads eventually to Ladywell Chapel at Fernyhalgh. There has probably been a trackway along here for many centuries but it was not until enclosure in 1817 that a road was laid out. In the distance is Killinscough Farm, a very old enclosure dating back to the fourteenth century when it was referred to as 'Kylaneshalghe'. In recent years, contractors working on road construction uncovered a burial ditch containing hundreds of human skeletons on land near to the farm. (From *R. Cunliffe-Shaw, The Royal Forest of Lancaster*)

roads opened up previously inaccessible corners of Fulwood which, in time, would become the farthest reaches of suburbia. In some cases this was not for many years – for example, the Long Sands Lane area, which consisted of a handful of farms for nearly two hundred years. In the 1970s the Central Lancashire Development Corporation put forward housing schemes which would use this 'green belt' land. Now, the old lane is almost unrecognisable and a new route carries traffic to a motorway junction. The farmland has recently become a maze of newly-built closes and cul-de-sacs. This was one of the last unspoilt parts of old Fulwood Moor.

Farmhouses and cottages

Clock House Farm, at the northern end of Fulwood Row, was rebuilt in the eighteenth century, replacing the original structure which, it is said, was burnt down during the years of religious persecution. Earlier that century, it was the home of Christopher Wadsworth, one of the family from Haighton Hall, known

79

Catholic recusants, whose estates were sequestrated after the 1715 Uprising.

The new building was built in a style quite revolutionary for its time. The brick-built house was 'boxy' in shape and two rooms thick, which enabled the builder to plan the interior better and incorporate fireplaces and a staircase in the most convenient position. Clock House is quite a common name in rural areas.

My Uncles Farm on Midgery Lane was demolished in 1980 and an extensive survey of the farmhouse and outbuildings at the time revealed a history going back centuries. It was not a grand farmhouse and was probably tenanted for all of its existence, as periodic refurbishment and extensions had obviously been done on a limited budget. At its core was a sixteenth-century cruck frame which would have supported a single-storey dwelling constructed with wattle and daub walls and a thatched roof. Even this structure was probably not the first on the site and, at the time of construction, was a fairly substantial dwelling, indicating

Clock House Farm. Fulwood Row. The earliest reference to Clock House is in 1703 when it was occupied by Christopher Wadsworth, a relation of the family living in Haighton Hall. They were known Catholic recusants and it is said that the original house was burnt down in penal times. This house was built at the end of the eighteenth century and is marked clearly on Yates' Map of 1786. (*Reproduced by kind permission of the Commission for the New Towns*, ref. NTC 35/2/159)

My Uncles Farm, Midgery Lane, which was demolished in 1980. Before the bulldozers moved in a detailed survey was undertaken at the site. At the core of this dilapidated farmhouse was a sixteenth-century cruck frame, dating the building back to the Tudor Period. Whilst little was left of the original structure its existence proved that this part of Fulwood Moor was inhabited hundreds of years ago. In fact references to 'Miggenrow' go back to the fifteenth century.

Barn at My Uncles Farm. My Uncles Farm was part of the Broughton Tower estate. The large pieces of stone used in the construction of this barn were thought to have been reclaimed from the Tower itself which was demolished around 1800. (*Photographs reproduced by kind permission of the Commission for the New Towns*)

that the occupant was secure in his tenure from the Singletons of Broughton Tower.

When brick became more widely used in the eighteenth century, the walls were rebuilt and the living quarters rearranged with the addition of a new fireplace. A second storey and an

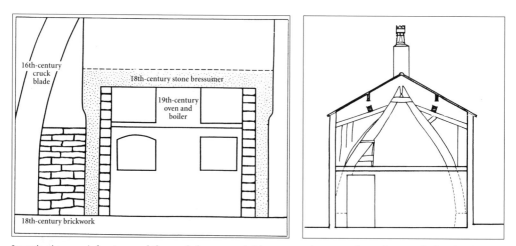

Investigations carried out around the cruck frame revealed how successive generations of tenants had updated the farmhouse with the addition of brick in the eighteenth century; an internal fireplace in the eighteenth century; followed by a nineteenth century oven and boiler. Variations in the external brickwork also showed that the house had originally been a single storey structure which was later extended to two. (*Reproduced by kind permission of the Commission for the New Towns*)

internal staircase were added at that time. In the old days the livestock had shared the single dwelling with the family, but a new substantial barn was then built with stones thought to have come from the recently demolished Broughton Tower.

But how did it come by its unusual name? It was said that a nephew when asked at a meeting to supply the name of the farm could only reply: 'We call it 'My Uncles'', but he never did know the true name. Neither is it possible to identify the long line of inhabitants. The initials RPA were carved into a lintel dated 1791. Did they belong to one of the Arkwright family who are known to have lived thereabouts and had 'a close of land called Miggen-row' in the fifteenth century? These are mysteries which will probably never be solved.

The Tannery, also on Midgery Lane, is a legacy from Fulwood's years of farming. It nestled in a hollow by the Savick Brook, from which it drew the copious quantities of water needed for the tanning pits. Before steam power, horses played an important role in industry and leather was in demand for equipment such as harnesses, belts and for clothing and shoes. Hides were soaked for up to a year in a specially-prepared tanning solution, made from oak bark, before being passed to the currier for finishing.

To be Sold,
BY AUCTION
BY MR. SAMUEL PARKER,
(OF FARRINGTON,)

AT THE HOUSE OF

Mr. Jno. Leeming,
SAWYERS' ARMS, SNOW HILL, PRESTON,
On TUESDAY, SEPTEMBER 30th, 1851,
AT SIX O'CLOCK P.M.,

THE

FEE-SIMPLE AND INHERITANCE
OF AN

ESTATE

Called "MY UNCLE'S,"
Containing 61a. 1r. 4p., of LAND,
Statute Measure, or thereabouts,

Situate in the Township of BROUGHTON, about Two and a half Miles from Preston, and is within a few minutes' walk of Fernyhalgh Chapel, and Broughton Church.

A considerable portion of the Land has been thoroughly drained, and the whole possesses every qualification desirable for a Milk Farm.

Conditions will be produced at the time of Sale; and any further information may be obtained from Mr. GEORGE SINGLETON, Land Surveyor, at Mr. HUNT'S Office, Chapel Walks, Preston, and of Mr. RICHARD GORNALL, Broughton Tower, Broughton; and, for to view the Premises application may be made to THOMAS KELLETT, the present Tenant.

Broughton, 19th Sep., 1851.

CLARKE, PRINTER, PILOT-OFFICE, 37, FISHERGATE, PRESTON.

Sale bill for My Uncle's Farm.

The importance of this ancient skill is revealed in the Guild Rolls of past centuries. For example, in the year 1622, 42 of the total 158 burgesses were recorded as being in leather-related trades.

In eighteenth-century Fulwood, farm incomes were often supplemented by other labours such as weaving. The mechanisation of the spinning process was well under way by the end of the

The Tannery. Midgery Lane. Known originally as the Tan Pits which were the large holes in the ground where the hides were soaked. Apparently, the tanning solution was a specially prepared cocktail of unpleasant smelling ingredients, so tanneries were usually found in isolated locations and downwind of any neighbours.

Sharoe Green Lane. In 1817, the enclosure commissioners extended Sharoe Green Lane south to connect to Watling St Road. Previously it had petered out just near this bridge crossing the Savick Brook. This short section of the old lane has survived the widening scheme of the 1970s. The new road, now a busy access route to the Royal Preston Hospital, can be seen to the left of the photograph.

century, but weaving was still done on a handloom by operatives working in their own home. The spun yarn was delivered to the weavers by the manufacturer, who collected the finished cloth to be taken to market. Fulwood's close proximity to the spinning

Shire Bank Hall. This nineteenth-century country house on Sharoe Green Lane was originally part of the Derby estate. The first occupant was a gentleman farmer called John Ingham who lived there with his wife and four children. The house was demolished in the 1980s and replaced with Sharoe Mount Court, a development of retirement flats.

mills assured the outworkers of a constant supply of yarn and people welcomed the extra income to supplement the unreliable profits from the land. Suprisingly, this situation lasted well into the nineteenth century, but once power looms took over, the factory system rapidly replaced the home-based industry. The census return for the year 1841 listed nearly a quarter of the

85

population of Fulwood as weavers. At Windy Nook, just north of Withy Trees, there were six cottages, owned by Abraham Sedgwick of Larch House, all occupied by weavers.

Shire Bank Farm and Greystocks Cottages. The tenant farmers on the west side of Sharoe Green Lane would have farmed land belonging to Lord Derby. Shire Bank Farm with its extensive outbuildings, and Greystocks Cottages are reminders of the area's rural past.

These two farm cottages on Longsands Lane have survived the development of recent years and are a reminder of the area's agricultural past.

Springfield Cottage and Holderness House. Typical of the older properties on Black Bull Lane. In the nineteenth century, they were surrounded by orchards. Marston's Farm fronting the bend of the Old Lancaster Lane had over four acres of fruit trees and gave its name to Orchard Court which was built on the land.

Road names recalling the past

Following the enclosure of Fulwood and Cadley Moors the whole district had to be reassessed for Church Tithes. Fulwood was still beholden to Lancaster parish for this annual tax, based on assessment of £300. Every plot of land was valued and listed and in 1848 the new schedules and maps were issued by the Tithe Commissioners. They provide a complete picture of Fulwood and Cadley Moors in early Victorian times, with every landholding, boundary, farm house, cottage, barn, garden and so on, described, together with its value and the names of the owners and occupiers. This was just before modern Fulwood was built, around the Garstang Road and Watling Street Road developments. A study of this map reminds us that most of old Fulwood has now disappeared.

In the Cadley Causeway area the only house still standing is Cadley Bank House in Cadley Drive, but in 1848 there were others whose names have been used for the new roads built on their sites – 'The Filberts', owned by Thomas Lythcoe, Laurel Bank, Dunkirk House and Millbank, for example, whilst Mill Lane recalls the ancient corn-mill.

The twentieth-century road names 'Saxon Hey' and 'Athelstan Fold' are remarkable in that they hark back to the previous millenium. There was indeed a hey thereabouts in Saxon times called the Hey of Mamegil, which is listed as part of the ancient boundaries of Fulwood Forest. A hey was a clearing in the forest where stray animals were rounded up, and Mamegil was the name of the man who owned the hey.

'Athelstan Fold', also a Saxon name, recalls King Athelstan who purchased the whole of Amounderness in which Cadley stands, and in AD 930 gave it to the parish of St Peter in York. It is quite likely that he travelled through this district on his journey from Eamont-bridge in Cumbria to North Wales in AD 927 – an interesting connection!

There have been two Seymour Roads. The first one ran a short distance from the humpbacked railway bridge alongside Savick Brook. When the Tomlinson estate on the south side of the brook was developed, the new Lytham Road was cut through to Woodplumpton Road. The old name was used again when the land on the north bank of the brook was built upon more recently.

In the Black Bull Lane area – then called Old Lancaster Turnpike Lane – we see Windsor House which gave its name to Windsor Drive, and, following that, to a succession of Royal 'Drives' – Princes, Queens, Kings and Regent.

Boys and Walker Lane recall the two families who lived at Ingolhead, whilst Scotts Wood stands on Scott's Farm land, and 'The Turnpike' is but a stone's throw from where young William Alston collected dues at the toll-gate.

On the eastern side of Garstang Road, Greystock Ave and Shire Bank Crescent are both named after nearby old farmhouses. Fulwood Hall Lane runs up to the old hall now Preston Golf Club's clubhouse, whilst Singleton Lane and Tower Lane are on the land of Broughton Tower, ancient home of the Singletons.

Gamull Lane is named after Sir Francis Gamull of Cheshire who in past centuries owned the property there. He married one of the Houghton family of Lea.

A Victorian mansion gave its name to Highgate Avenue, and later to an estate which was built on the site of the old house, whilst Manor Avenue is built on the land which the Enclosure Commissioner, William Miller, purchased for his manor house. Later he built Clayton Villa on the high ground off Sharoe Green Lane.

Sherwood is named after a nursery which was situated at the end of Sharoe Mount Avenue. Joseph Walmsley started the business after the Great War, in which he fought with the Sherwood Foresters Unit, 11th Battalion. He named his market gardening business Sherwood Nurseries in memory of his war time unit.

The story of the naming of another drive in Fulwood provides a rather sad postscript. The houses on Aubigny Drive, off Black Bull Lane, were built just after the First World War for the Aikman family. A member of the family, Alec, had been killed and was buried in Aubigny in France, and the road was so named as a permanent memorial to him.

PRESTON RACES, 1830.

CLARKE'S — **CORRECT LIST.**

☞ *To start as soon as the Cockings are over.—The Races to be run in the order in which they are placed.*

On TUESDAY, JULY 13th, 1830, WILL BE RUN FOR ON FULWOOD MOOR,

The Fifth STANLEY STAKES of 10 sovs. each;
The Stanley Course (one mile and a quarter).—To this
Sweepstakes, 30 sovs will be added.

Mr. Simpson's b m The Duchess, 6 y o (Jaques)	1
Mr. Hopkinson's b g The Captain,	2
Mr. Clifton's b f Butterfly, 4 y o	3
Sir T. Stanley's b f Lady Constance,—purp & yel	0
Sir J. Gerard's br c bv Figaro, 3 y o	0
Mr. R. Turner's br h Olympus 5 y o—yel bod, blue sl	0
Ld Stanley's b c Felt, 4 y o	pd

The Captain the favorite, 6 to 1 on the field—the winner not mentioned, who took the lead, was never headed, and after a well contested race by the Captain, won by a neck.

Same day, PRODUCE STAKES of 50 sovs. each,
colts, 8st 5lb—fillies, 8st 2lb—untried stallions, &c.
allowed 3lb—one mile and three quarters.

Sir T. Stanley's b c Lawrie Todd, (Templeman)	1
Sir W. Wynne's bl f Georgiana,—crimson and wht.	2
Mr. Clifton's b c Buy-a-broom,	3
Ld Derby's b c Barometer, by Whisker—or	4
Ld Grosvenor's b f Frail, by Filho—orange, blk cp	4

Lawrie Todd the favourite—won in a canter.

Same day, £70. the gift of the Hon. E. G. Stanley and
J. Wood, Esq. Members for the Borough, for horses
&c. of all ages, that never won plate, match, or sweep-
stakes of the value of £50. before the day of entrance;
—heats, twice round and a distance—to start at the
distance chair. 10 sovs. will be paid to the second horse.

Mr. Skipsey's b c bv Whisker, (Holmes)	0 0 1 1
Mr. Moor's br c Bastard, 4 y o	0 1 0 2
Mr. Clifton's b c bv Antonio, 3 y o	0 2 2 dr
Mr. Teebay's b g Captain, aged—blue	0 0 0 dr
Mr. W. Turner's b f The Nab, 3 y o	0 0 dr
Mr. Nowell's b f by Ivanhoe, 3 y o	1 0 dr
Mr. Hardy's b m Cottage Girl, 5 y o	0 0 dr
Ld Sligo's b c Canker, 3 y o—crimson	dis

Canker came in first for first heat, but it was given to Mr Nowell's filly, in consequence of a jostle.

On WEDNESDAY the 14th, a Sweepstakes of 100
sovs. each, h ft.—8st 2lb—one mile and a distance.

Mr. Clifton's c f Moss Rose,—brown—walked over	
Lord Derby's c f Rose Leaf,—blk jacket, wht cp	pd
Mr. Nowell's br f by Orville,—rose	pd
Mr. Yates' br f Evelina, by Paulowitz—pur, & or cp	pd

Same day, a GOLD CUP, or Piece of Plate, value 100 sovs
added to a sweepstakes of 10 sovs. each; three years old,
6st 6lb—four, 8st—five, 8st 10lb—six and aged, 9st—the
winner of the Cup at Preston, in any year, to carry 5lbs.

Ld Derby's b c Felt, by Langar, 4 y o (Johnson)	1
Mr. Lomax's br c Guido, by Peter Lely, 4 y o—br	2
Sir T. Stanley's ch h May Fly, by Piscator, aged	pd
Mr. Wood's br c Voltaire, by Blacklock, 4 y o	pd
Mr. R. Wilbraham's c c Graudee, by Cervantes, 4 y o	pd
Mr. E. G. Stanley's c f Tib, by Langar, 4 y o	pd
Ld Wilton's b h Pelion, by Blacklock, 4 y o	pd
Mr. Clifton's br h Fylde, by Antonio, 6 y o	pd
Mr. Clifton's b c Lely, by Peter Lely, 4 y o	pd
Mr. Yates' br c Douglas, by Filho da Puta, 4 y o	pd
Major Yarburgh's b h Laurel, by Blacklock, 6 y o	pd
Mr. Petre's c c Rowton, by Oiseau, 4 y o	pd
Mr. S Reed's br c Wandering Boy, by Oiseau, 4 y	pd

Felt the favorite at very high odds—Won easy.

Same day, £70. given by the Right Hon. the Earl of
Derby; three years old, 7st 4lb—four, 8st 7lb—mares
and geldings allowed 3lb—maiden horses, &c. allowed
2lb—heats, one mile and a quarter. 10 sovs. will be
paid to the second horse.

Mr. Ferguson's b c Young Patrick, (Jaques)	4 4 1 1
Mr. Hopkinson's b g The Captain, 4 y o	1 2 2 2
Mr. Shepley's b c Catillus, 4 y o—harlequin	3 1 dis
Sir T. Mostyn's b f Sprig, 3 y o—yel and blk	2 5 dr
Mr. Simpson's br f Moll in-the-Wad, 4 y o	5 dr
Lord Derby's ch c Mirabel, 4 y o	6 3 dr

In consequence of a cross by Catillus, the third heat was given to Patrick.

Mr. W. Turner's b f The Nab, 3 y o	dr
Mr. Moor's br c Bastard, 4 y o—purp & yellow	dr
Mr. Skipsey's b c bv Whisker, 3 y o	dr
Mr. Nowell's b f by Ivanhoe, 3 y o—rose	dr
Mr. Nowell's b f by Walton, 4 y o—rose	dr
Sir J. Gerard's br c bv Figaro, 3 y o—br and yel	dr
Sir T. Stanley's b f Lady Constance, 3 y o	dr
Mr. Healey's b c Flambeau, 4 y o—purple	dr
Mr. Clifton's b f Butterfly, 4 y o—br and yel	dr
Mr. Clifton's b c bv Antonio, 3 y o—br and yel	dr

On FRIDAY the 16th, a Sweepstakes of 100 sovs.
each, h ft—One mile and a quarter.

Mr. Clifton's c f Moss Rose, 8st 7lb	walked over.
Ld Derby's g c Brother to Halston,—blk & wht cp	pd
Ld Grosvenor's b c Barometer, 8st 7lb—yel & blk	pd
Ld Grosvenor's b c Thermometer, 8st 4lb—same	pd
Sir T. Stanley's b c bv Whisker,—purp & yel	pd

Same day, a Sweepstakes of 15 sovs. each, 10 sovs. forfeit,
with £50 added (provided it is not walked over for) by
Mr. Scott, of the Bull Inn, for all ages; three years
old, 7st 2lb—four, 8st 5lb—five, 8st 10lb—six and aged,
9st—mares and geldings allowed 2lb—a winner of a
plate or stake of the value of £50. or upwards, in the
present year, to carry 5lb extra, of two or more, 7lb—
heats, one mile and a distance.

Mr Clifton's b f Butterfly, 4 y o (Nelson)	1 1
Mr Hopkinson's b g The Captain, 4 y o	3 2
Mr R. Turner's br h Olympus, 5 y o	2 dr
Lord Derby's c h Mirabel, 4 y o—blk & wht cp	pd

Same day, £70. for all ages; three years old, 6st 12lb
four, 8st—five, 8st 10lb—six and aged, 8st 12lb—mares
and geldings allowed 3lb—the winner of plate, match,
or sweepstakes, in the present year, to carry 3lb extra;
of two or more, 5lb, or the winner of the cup this year,
7lb extra—heats, two miles and a distance. 10 sovs. to
the second horse.

Mr. Ferguson's b c Young Patrick, (Jaques)	5 1 1
Mr. Shepley's b c Catillus, 4 y o—blue	1 3 2
Mr. R. Turner's b h Clinton, 5 y o—yel bod	6 2 4
Sir T. Mostyn's b f Regina, 3 y o	4 4 3
Mr. Simpson's b m Duchess, 6 y o—pur	2 dr
Mr. Clifton's b h Poor Fellow, 5 y o	3 dr
Mr. R. Turner's br h Olympus, 5 y o—yel bod, blue	dr
Sir T. Mostyn's b f Sprig, 3 y o—yel & blk cp	dr
Lord Derby's ch c Mirabel, 4 y o—blk, & wht cp	dr
Mr. Nowell's b f by Ivanhoe, 3 y o—rose	dr
Mr. Nowell's b f by Walton, 4 y o—rose	dr
Mr. Hopkinson's b g The Captain, 4 y o—str bod,	dr
Mr. Skipsey's b c bv Whisker, 3 y o—sky bl	dr
Mr. Clifton's b f Butterfly, 4 y o—br & yellow	dr
Mr. Clifton's b c bv Antonio, 3 y o—same	dr

ALEX. NOWELL, Esq. } STEWARDS.
JOHN LOMAX, Esq.

JOHN CATON, Clerk of the Course.

THE COCKINGS.

A Main of Cocks will be fought, commencing Monday the 12th, between the Earl of Derby, (Potter, feeder,) and Col. Yates, (Gilliver, feeder,) for 10 sovs. a battle, and 100 sovs. the main. 27 mains, 5 byes.

POTTER.	m.	b.	GILLIVER.	m.	b.
MONDAY	4	2	MONDAY	2	0
TUESDAY	3	1	TUESDAY	4	0
WEDNESDAY	3	0	WEDNESDAY	4	1
FRIDAY	6	1	FRIDAY	1	0
	16	4		11	1

No persons to ride within the cords except they belong to the Horses, or are authorised by the Stewards.—No person will be allowed to stand within the rails after the Bell rings, and any of the Staff-men neglecting to enforce this order, will be discharged.—All Dogs found on the Course will be destroyed.

CHAPTER SEVEN

The King's 96 Acres

T WAS STIPULATED in the Enclosure Award of 1811 that the King should retain a twelfth of the remaining commonland in Fulwood – ninety-six acres in total. It also stipulated that no road was to pass through this land, and it is because of this that Watling Street Road takes an otherwise unaccountable detour from its old Roman route. This last portion of Crown land was at the time leased to Edward Lord Stanley who, for some years, had been using it for a horse-racing course.

Horse racing was a popular sport with the gentry of Preston, but the reason for having two courses so close together, one on Fulwood Moor and one on Preston Moor, was the result of a political feud in the town. Race meetings had taken place on Preston moor (now Moor Park) as early as 1726. However, from 1786 to 1791 the meetings had to compete with rival events being held on Fulwood Moor by Lord Derby and his supporters. Meetings on Preston Moor ceased in 1791 but racing on Fulwood Moor remained popular for many more years. The highly-prized Gold Cup attracted a good turn-out each year and its most famous runner was Dr Syntax, who won the race seven times from 1815 to 1821.

Special meetings were held during Guild week and the following report was given in Wilcockson's 'Authentic Records of the Guild Merchant of Preston' for the year 1822:

Every description of vehicle was in requisition this morning to convey the influx of visitors to the races. During the forenoon the crowds of pedestrians that lined the road to the course on Fulwood Moor was immense. By 2 o'clock, the time when the horses started, there was grand display of splendid equipages, all arrayed in new liveries. The ladies' stand and the grand-stand were both fitted up for the occasion and well attended, and there was no want of temporary places for refreshment, where the honest countryman and the industrious mechanic, quaffed the nut brown ale, for which Preston has always been famous.

A large importation of gentlemen black legs had raised various temples of fortune to seduce the unwary into the mysteries of the iniquitous vice of gambling.

The weather was most unfavourable to the sport; a heavy rain continued almost from the commencement of the first race, and many a holiday suit bore evident marks of the leng-thened way and dirty road, on their way home.

Fulwood race course ran its last meeting in 1833, when the Earl of Derby moved from the town after a political defeat.

The King's land was bounded on the south side by the newly constructed Watling Street Road. Along this section of road was a row of cottages known as 'the booths'. These were the homes of poor farm labourers who tended the cattle grazing on the land. They were often known as 'boothies' or 'boothmen' and were employed by a keeper who leased both the stock and land for the land owner. This system of farm, known as a vaccary, was quite common in the Royal forests. The keeper would receive 'lactage' (a proportion of the milk yield) which he could use himself or sell. The boothmen were given little more than a roof over their heads.

In 1822, Earl Stanley's lease was transferred to William Miller, the Enclosure Commissioner, who built a house at the western end of the site called the Manor House. The property, approached from a gate on Watling St Road, was demolished around 1910 and replaced with the houses on Manor Avenue and Duchy Avenue. William Miller did not stay long in his Manor House because soon after it was built plans for a military barracks on Fulwood's Crown land were under discussion. The original suggestion of a site in Blackburn had been abandoned, leaving Fulwood as the only other likely location. The Lancashire indus-trial towns were certainly in need of a strong military presence to quell the industrial unrest which centred on the cotton mills.

Rioting gangs protesting against poor working conditions and low pay were becoming regular occurrences.

The impact of such a large military establishment on Fulwood could not be underestimated, but the land was ideally situated and seemed destined for this use. Mr Miller did not, however, leave the area. He rented another prime piece of building land from the Claytons and built himself a new home called Clayton Villa. The house, on the hill at the eastern side of Sharoe Green Lane, not far from its junction with Watling Street Road, has one of the finest uninterrupted views across Preston Golf Club, an outlook which has changed little from the time when it was part of the manorial estate of the Clayton family.

Fulwood Barracks

During the summer of 1998 Fulwood Barracks commemorated its opening one hundred and fifty years before. Its purpose initially was to house troops which could be called upon to quell unrest locally but, over its long history, it has played an important role in many famous campaigns and world wars.

Quite a different Fulwood surrounds this once isolated hilltop location, now the busy junction of Watling Street Road and Sir Tom Finney Way (formerly known as Deepdale Road). Years before the military took up residence, the site of the barracks was a hive of activity. Preparatory work started in July 1842 and the following August the first stone was officially laid at a small ceremony. Fortunately, the Preston to Longridge Railway had just opened and could transport the huge quantities of stone for its construction from quarries near Longridge. The line, until 1848, was worked entirely by horses and built solely to meet the increased demand for stone used for many public buildings. The barracks took five years to build, providing employment for three to four hundred labourers and, on completion, the final cost of the project was calculated to the farthing – a total of £137,921 2s. 10d., approximately £300 over the estimated sum.

Fulwood Barracks was constructed on a grand scale, giving the soldiers a standard of accommodation which surpassed any previously afforded to the military. It was certainly the largest ever built in the North of England. The principal entrance, originally

Below: Fulwood Barracks *c.*1900. One man and his dog standing near the original barracks gateway. The historic archway was demolished in 1960 and the Royal Arms, which was sculpted from a solid block of stone, placed on the lawn to the left of the entrance.

through a massive gateway surmounted with the royal arms, was demolished in the 1960s and the coat of arms placed on the lawn nearby. This has opened up the approach road and exposed the attractive chapel building which is supported on eight pillars forming an archway through to the square.

This postcard was entitled 'Sunday morning at the entrance of Fulwood Barracks'. The little girl in the centre of the pathway appears undeterred by the crowds of men lining the road. The reason for this big turnout is not known; perhaps they waiting to greet a visitor to the barracks.

During the First World War, Fulwood Soldiers Welfare Committee ran this café for the troops. On the menu: tea, coffee and buns, a half-penny; sandwiches and aerated waters, one penny.

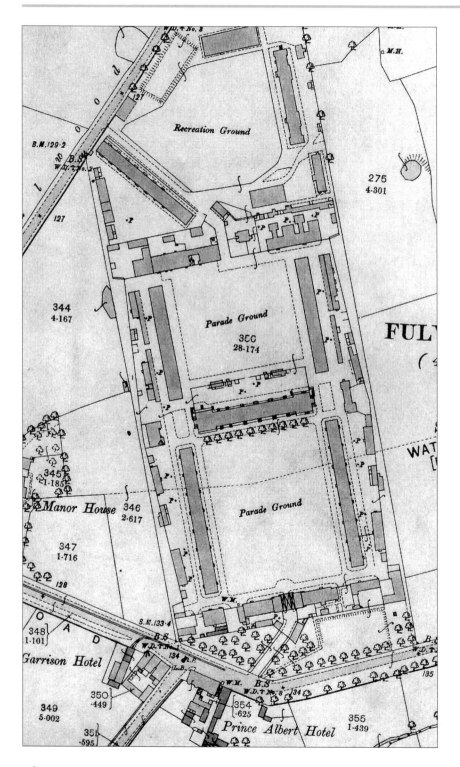

Summer's Hotel, 1985, shortly before its demolition to allow an improvement in the Deepdale Road/Watling Street Road junction. Originally known as the Prince Albert Hotel, this old hostelry was a popular venue for officers at the barracks. Some even took up permanent residence in one of the rooms above the bar. Its most famous guest was Padre George Smith who's bravery at Rouke's Drift in the face of four thousand Zulus was commemorated in the film *Zulu*.

Inside, the buildings were arranged around two parade grounds – the Infantry Square and the Cavalry Square, each flanked by two-storey stone terraces where ordinary soldiers were once housed. Across the centre of the site were the officers' quarters and here no expense was spared in furnishing them to the highest standards. Unlike the troops, who slept in dormitories, the officers had their own private apartments and access to a 'well-fitted kitchen' and 'elegant mess rooms'. The list of 'on site' amenities was endless; the barracks had its own hospital, prison, school and library, along with numerous workshops where military equipment was manufactured.

The completion of the barracks in June 1848 was closely followed by the opening of two hostelries on Watling Street Road. The Garrison Hotel and The Sumners were well used by their military neighbours, both for off-duty refreshment and for officers' accommodation. Some years ago, a tunnel was uncovered in the cellar of The Garrison which led underneath the road to the barracks, but the reason for its existence never came to light. The old Sumners was demolished in 1985 to make room for a slip road to ease traffic congestion. It had originally been called

the Prince Albert Hotel, but later took the name of one of its owners, William Sumner. He built up the business by operating a brewery at the rear of the premises, from where he also ran a livery stables. The barracks residents were regular customers of Mr Sumner's enterprises and when he died in 1914, he had accumulated a small fortune.

One of the Sumners Hotel's most famous residents was Padre George Smith, who was Barracks Chaplain from 1899 to 1903. He is remembered for his outstanding bravery in the defence of Rourke's Drift by one hundred British soldiers against nearly four thousand Zulus, as portrayed in the film *Zulu*. Rev. Smith was a resident at The Sumners from 1905 to 1918. He died there on 27 November 1918 at the age of 73 and is buried in Preston Cemetery.

The first troops to arrive at Fulwood Barracks were the 2nd Battalion 60th Rifles, followed by the Loyal Lincoln Volunteers on 17 May 1848. This was the start of a regimental connection

Deepdale Road around 1930. Even then this was becoming a busy junction and required this road widening construction to ease traffic problems. The old Sumner's Hotel can be seen, with the Barracks beyond. (Reproduced by kind permission of the Lancashire Evening Post)

which lasts to the present day. In 1881, following a regimental reorganisation, the Volunteers were redesignated as 1st and 2nd Battalions of the Loyal North Lancashire Regiment. They were joined at Fulwood in 1898 by the East Lancashire Regiment, who had had to move from Burnley Barracks because it was in a poor state of repair. These two regiments remained together for over forty years, their main peacetime function being to train recruits, but, through the Boer War and both World Wars, they received and equipped troops before being posted. When conscription was introduced in 1939 it was necessary to provide more living accommodation so wooden huts were erected over the whole of the North Cavalry Square. The fields to the north of the site, once exercise areas for horses, were used in the 1960s for the building of modern married quarters.

There have been many dramatic incidents in the barracks' long history but none more famous that the shooting of two officers in 1861 by Private Patrick McCaffrey. He was apparently a troublesome soldier who, on this particular day, reluctantly carried out an order to reprimand some children who were suspected of breaking windows. His failure to carry out the duty successfully resulted in a sentence from Colonel Crofton to be confined to barracks for fourteen days. Later that day, McCaffrey saw two officers (one of whom was Colonel Crofton) walking across the square, took his rifle and fired. Both officers were seen to stagger and fall and it was discovered that the bullet had passed through Colonel Crofton's lungs and then through the chest of Captain Hanham, resulting in their deaths. McCaffrey was arrested and charged with their murder. His only plea of defence was that he had been the victim of Hanham's tyranny and revenge had led him to commit the crime. He was hanged in January 1862, but many would say that his unhappy spirit still haunts the premises; several accounts of ghostly sightings at Fulwood Barracks have been recorded in the past.

Information taken from the census returns reveals that the population of Fulwood in the years between 1841 and 1851 increased by over 1000, due almost entirely to the opening of Fulwood Barracks. It was a great change to this quiet rural community and inevitably caused some problems. For example, reports by the Local Board of Health often mentioned the pollution of the waterways taking the sewerage from the barracks. This became much more acute after 1851 when suburban development started to bring more people to the area. However, in time, the barracks became part of the local community which grew up around it. Local householders were able to generate extra income by providing accommodation for officers stationed in Fulwood and, undoubtedly, many romances blossomed between local girls and handsome young soldiers. Sadly, not all had a happy ending. One of the entries in the police log book in August 1887 was an incident involving a servant girl called Alice Maud Farrell who had run away with her soldier boyfriend dressed in clothes stolen from her mistress. Her foolhardy measure to impress her young man was discovered, and on returning to Fulwood, Alice was arrested and sentenced to six weeks hard labour. There are no doubt many more tales to tell of this historic military station.

CHAPTER EIGHT

A Home in the Suburbs

The Country Houses of Fulwood

The population of Fulwood at the turn of the nineteenth century was around 400 and by 1841 had increased to 628; but this small growth in population appeared to have little to do with farming. The census return of 1841 revealed a number of recently built country houses occupied by professional and independently wealthy members of the community. New roads had improved access to Preston, and Fulwood was becoming a popular location for a 'country residence'. Wealth, generated from the successes of the early cotton manufactories, was financing the aspirations of the self-made man who, learning quickly from the landed gentry, sought a life-style in keeping with his newly acquired affluence.

Greyfriars and Uplands Hall on Walker Lane

To the present day, Walker Lane has retained the charm and character of a country backwater as it winds it way from Black Bull Lane to Lightfoot Lane. It was chosen by several Victorian families as the perfect spot for their 'out of town' residence.

Perhaps the finest example still standing is Greyfriars, about half a mile along the lane, built for James Clayton, an ironfounder. In 1839 he was living in a house called Broughton Bank which stood a little to the north of Greyfriars. In 1849 he commissioned the building of his new property, where he resided until his death in 1885. The house was then sold to Frank Hollins who considerably enlarged it and laid out the grounds with formal pathways, shrubbery and flower beds. The garden became a showpiece and to the present day is lovingly tended by its owners who

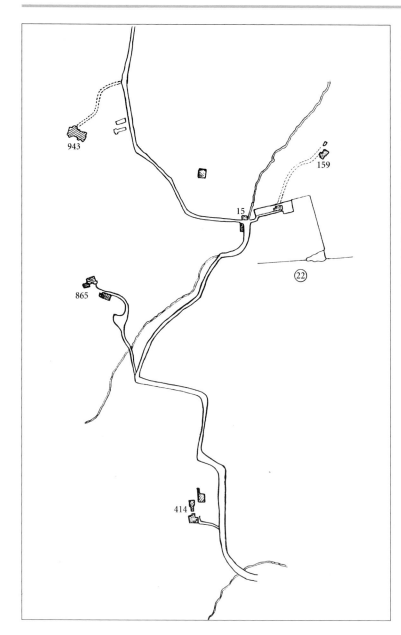

A sketch map of Walker Lane based on the Tithe Map of Broughton, 1839.

Key:

159 – House owned by James Clayton.

15 – House owned by Ellen Beesley.

22 – Tan pit field.

28 – Cottage and garden.

943 – House and pleasure grounds owned by Lieut.-Gen. Sir Thomas Whitehead.

865 – House owned by James Teebay.

414 – House owned by Alexander Haliburton.

occasionally open it to the public. Mr Hollins became head of Horrocks, Crewdson & Co., one of Preston's largest cotton manufacturing firms. He was also a lifelong member of the Liberal Party. His great love was cricket and he became a keen supporter of Lancashire County Club, which he assisted in its move to the Old Trafford ground. In 1907, he was included in the King's

Opposite: A plan of the Greyfriars estate from the Sale Catalogue of 1924.

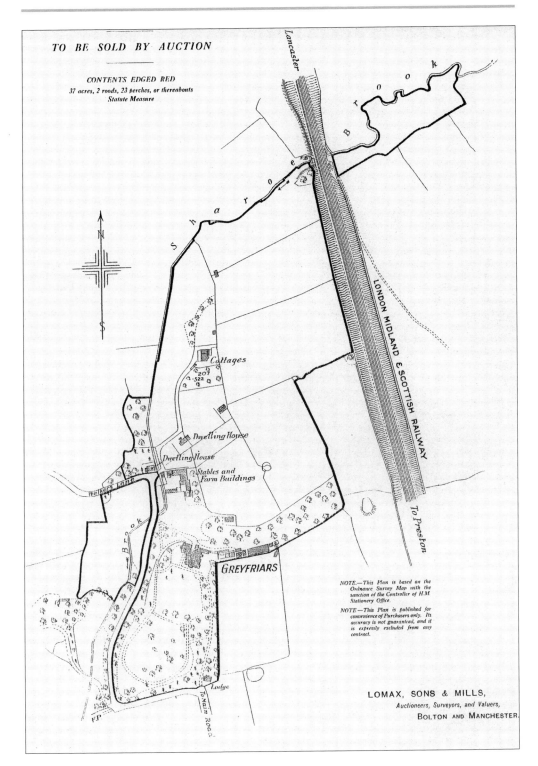

TO BE SOLD BY AUCTION

CONTENTS EDGED RED
37 acres, 2 roods, 23 perches, or thereabouts
Statute Measure

Lancaster

London Midland & Scottish Railway

To Preston

N

S

S h a r o e B r o o k

F.B.

Cottages
207
·522

Dwelling House
Dwelling House
Stables and
Farm Buildings

Walker's Lane

Brook

GREYFRIARS

NOTE.—This Plan is based on the
Ordnance Survey Map with the
sanction of the Controller of H.M.
Stationery Office.

NOTE—This Plan is published for
convenience of Purchasers only. Its
accuracy is not guaranteed, and it
is expressly excluded from any
contract.

Lodge

To Main Road

LOMAX, SONS & MILLS,
Auctioneers, Surveyors, and Valuers,
BOLTON AND MANCHESTER.

Greyfriars, Walker Lane, 1924. This fine country residence was designed for a high society life-style. Additions to the four main reception rooms included a billiard room, entertaining rooms and lounge hall. The house had five servants bedrooms; a servants hall, extensive kitchen areas and four wine cellars. The gardens covered thirteen acres; within which there was a five car garage, squash racket court, tennis courts and stables. The house and home farm were sold by auction in 1924 after the death of Sir Frank Hollins.

Greyfriars, Walker Lane. (*Photograph courtesy of Mr & Mrs W. Harrison*)

birthday Honours List and named as Preston's new Baronet, Sir Frank Hollins, Bart ... There was a cricket ground at Greyfriars where English Electric Co. (now British Aerospace) used to play cricket league matches.

Another Victorian country house called Uplands Hall stood further along Walker Lane, but unfortunately the house was demolished and only the coach house remains. The hall was the home of Lieutenant-General Thomas Whitehead who was made a Knight after distinguished service in the East Indies. After his death in 1851 the hall was tenanted and eventually sold in 1886 to a bank manager, Colonel Oliver. Recently an estate of houses has been built on part of the site and it has been named after the grand old house and pleasure grounds of Uplands Hall.

Cadley Cottage

In the eighteenth century at the western end of Cadley Causeway there stood amongst open fields an old house called Cadley

Cottage. This was the summer home of one of Preston's most notable men, Nicholas Grimshaw, who served the town of Preston for the whole of his long life. His town house on Church Street gave its name to Grimshaw Street and later he bought an impressive house at the end of Winckley Street on Winckley Square, but Cadley Cottage was where he and his wife Esther spent their rare leisure hours.

Uplands Hall, Walker Lane, *c.* 1850. The upper floor was later dismantled, leaving a more balanced two-storey house. (*Reproduced courtesy of Lancashire County Library*)

Cadley Cottage, Cadley Causeway *c.* 1900. A sketch of Nicholas Grimshaw's country retreat as shown in Hewitson's *Northward*. Mrs Grimshaw called the cottage her 'Cadley Nest' and sought its solitude after her family bereavements.

He was seven times Mayor of Preston, twice Guild Mayor, clerk to the borough magistrates for over forty years, and for fifty years acting Cursitor for the County of Lancaster. He lived for eighty years and through some troubled times. When, in 1797, there was a threat of the invasion of England by the French, he founded and commanded for many years the Royal Volunteers,

Nicholas Grimshaw of Cadley Cottage 1758–1838. Commanding Officer of the Preston Volunteer Corps whose officers presented this portrait to his wife Esther Mary in the year 1802 when he was Guild Mayor.

a corps of men pledged to defend the town of Preston and the surrounding countryside.

His private life was greatly saddened by the death of four sons. The eldest boy, William, a Lieutenant in the 76th Regiment of Foot, was killed at the Isle aux Noix in Canada in 1815, and a young son died in infancy. In 1822, just as Nicholas was about to serve as Guild Mayor for the second time, a tragedy occurred which affected the whole town. Four young men, Nicholas and George Grimshaw, Henry Hulton and Joseph Kay, all under twenty one, were drowned in a boating accident in the River Ribble. It was reported that 'the Guild Mayoress-elect, Mrs Esther Grimshaw was too badly affected by the loss of her boys to appear as Guild Mayoress, so her place was taken by a married daughter Mrs Atkinson'. One can imagine that she would retreat to Cadley in her grief, for privacy from the Guild throngs. She loved the old cottage which she called her 'Cadley nest', and when her husband died in 1838, made it her home for the remaining fifteen years of her life, being cared for by two faithful family servants.

Cadley Bank

'Cadley Bank' was originally a detached cottage, probably built about 1800, facing the end of Cadley Causeway on Woodplumpton Road, built on land owned by Nicholas Grimshaw. Successive

Cadley Bank. c 1900.
Reproduced from
A. Hewitson's *Northward*.

Cadley Bank. 1997. Cadley Bank once stood in extensive gardens with a croquet lawn and coach house. Now surrounded by its more modern neighbours, it is easy to forget its illustrious past.

owners in the nineteenth century – Mr Simpson, Walter Platt, a woollen draper, Mr J. C. Welch, tea and coffee merchant, and Mr J. J. Smith, hatter, all Preston tradesmen – extended and improved the property which in 1821 could be described as ' the residence of a genteel family'. In 1872 Mr Smith purchased Cadley Bank and shortly afterwards enlarged the house, reordered the grounds and built a series of outbuildings at the rear. He turned the old house into an impressive villa standing in a large garden with a carriage drive sweeping from the gateway on Woodplumpton Road up to the front door. Behind the house was a large croquet lawn and a block of outbuildings which was bigger than the house itself.

The coachman had a coach-house, stables for the horses and his own forge. There was a house for the gardener, two conservatories, a potting shed, a peach house and a big vinery. At the back was a boiler-house, tool house and wash-house. In the twentieth century, when Woodplumpton Road was developed, all the grounds and outbuildings disappeared. The house still stands in Cadley Drive, now surrounded by modern housing built on the old gardens, croquet lawn and orchards. It is the only one of the old properties on the Cadley Causeway side of Fulwood to survive.

Oak House

North of Watling Street Road, on the eastern side of Garstang Road, is a portion of land which in the nineteenth century was owned by the Pedder family. In 1830 it was divided and sold to James Dandy and James Goodair. The land lay alongside the newly-constructed section of road from Withy Trees to the Black Bull and Mr Dandy, who was a builder, recognising the potential of his plot, set about building a fine mansion. Oak House was completed around 1840 and remained the home of the Dandy family for many years. It is now Saint Pius X Kindergarten and Preparatory School. Although modern extensions have been made, the original old house is virtually unaltered at the centre of the school.

Oak house *c.* 1950. The last private owner of Oak House was Mr H. F. Stenning, former director of North End Football Club. St Pius X School, who now occupy the house, started in Moor Park Avenue, then moved to the old St Vincent's Boy's School before buying Oak House around 1960. (*Reproduced with the permission of Lancashire Evening Post*)

Highgate Park

James Goodair never built on his portion and when he died in 1873 it was purchased by James Gregson, who in 1876 built Highgate Park, a splendid Victorian Gothic house. The Gregsons were an old Preston family who had invested wisely in the cotton industry and acquired great wealth. They appeared in the Guild Rolls in the eighteenth century and in 1702 Josiah Gregson became Guild mayor. The manufacturing business was founded by James's father at a small workshop in Marsh Lane. Here he produced spinning machinery for the production of cotton thread; but when mechanised weaving was introduced, James Gregson was quick to invest in the production of the new power-looms under a company called Gregson and Monk.

Highgate Park became the family home and James, who later became one of the largest property owners in Preston, took an active part in Fulwood affairs as a member of the district council.

Highgate Park. *c.* 1900. The home of James Gregson, wealthy machine manufacturer, built in 1876. The house remained in the family until it was demolished in the 1950s. (*Photographs courtesy of the Gregson family*)

James Gregson (1833–1906), at home in the garden of Highgate Park.

A small corner of his estate was leased to the tennis club of which he was a founder member.

James and his wife Alice had three sons and two daughters, and the eldest, John James, continued to live in Fulwood after the death of his father in 1906. Highgate Park remained the Gregson family home until 1957 when it was sold and later demolished. The interior of this great Victorian home was recorded at the turn of the century. The photographs captured the lavish decoration of high-Victorian style, furnished with an

Highgate Park taken from a plane in the 1940s. The old house was demolished in the 1950s and a housing estate was built on the land. The course of the Savick Brook is clearly defined running through the field. This area was subject to regular flooding after heavy rain, and some years ago a flood management scheme was constructed. A Victorian pathway through the woodland still exists and makes a pleasant walk connecting the end of Highgate Close to Foregate.

expensive collection of artefacts and paintings. In the 1950s when land for house building was at a premium, a plan to demolish Highgate Park for residential redevelopment was passed. The accumulated possessions of three generations were removed from the house and part of Fulwood's history was reduced to rubble. The old house is remembered in the naming of the estate which took its place.

Previous pages: The interior of Highgate Park was a perfect example of high Victorian style. Mr Gregson was a keen collector and the house was filled with expensive ornaments and paintings.

Altadore on Fulwood Row

Fulwood Row was the location chosen by William Philip Park for his country home called Altadore. A civil engineer and high ranking member of the Preston Conservative party, William Park was a very wealthy and influential member of the community. Altadore was designed for him in the late 1860s, in a style suitable for a country gentleman; it was a traditional house, where the family could live in privacy and friends could be entertained.

William and his wife Kathleen were in their early thirties when they moved into their new home with their young son, Philip.

Altadore. Fulwood Row. The Victorian home of William Philip Park is now occupied by Highfield Priory School, which moved from 'The Priory' on Lower Bank Road around 1980. The extensive grounds of the house (right) has given the school ample room to expand its facilities.

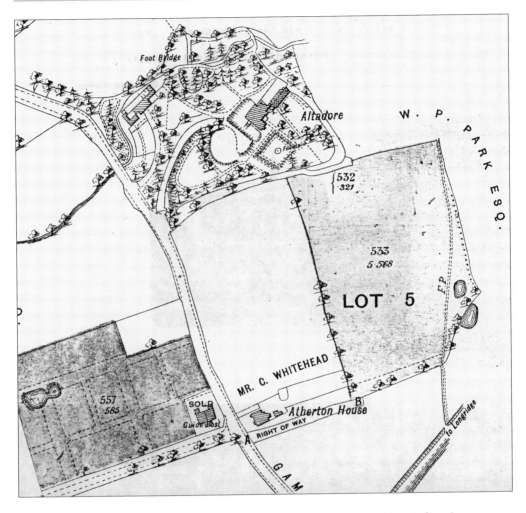

The family were comfortably outnumbered by six live-in servants: a cook, domestic servant, nurse, a young page, and two gardeners who lived in the cottage at the bottom of the garden. The house was approached by a gracious sweeping drive and surrounded by carefully tended gardens which sloped down to a brook. Sitting proudly on its elevated site, Altadore must have looked quite imposing.

The house is now occupied by Highfield Priory School and, although some of the grounds have been built on, the facade of the old house looks much as it did when Mr Park took up his residence in the last century. The old gardener's cottage, which pre-dates the Victorian house, still sits in the hollow by the stream.

Nestling in the hollow by the brook is the gardener's cottage to Altadore. There has been a cottage on this site for at least two hundred years which must have become part of the estate when Mr Park built Altadore.

CHAPTER NINE

Victorian Fulwood

Suburban villas, highway-side retreats,
That dread the encroachment of our growing streets,
Tight boxes, neatly sash'd, and in a blaze
With all a July sun's collected rays,
Delight the citizen, who, gasping there,
Breathes clouds of dust, and calls it country air.

William Cowper

NE OF THE MAJOR FACTORS which encouraged development in Victorian Fulwood was the deteriorating living conditions in Preston. The rapid expansion of the cotton industry resulted in a huge rise in the population from about 12,000 in 1801 to nearly 70,000 in 1851. A constant flow of people into the town put accommodation at a premium, giving unscrupulous landlords the excuse to charge high rents to prospective tenants desperate for a home. The town also had no planning or building regulations, resulting in cramped, poorly-constructed accommodation which was totally inadequate. It was not long before the consequences of this uncontrolled expansion were felt, destroying as it did the fabric of a fine market town, reducing it to a spread of 'industrial squalor' for which it became notorious.

Poor living conditions inevitably led to a high mortality rate which prompted numerous reports on the health and welfare of the town's working community. Their findings were alarming. In 1842, Revd. J. Clay, in his *Report on the Sanitary Conditions of Preston*, gave graphic descriptions of the appalling state of the slums: 'With no sewerage system in place, cesspools, which received the contents of the privies and drains as well as ashes and

Garstang Road, Preston.

refuse ran the length of the street'. The odour from this and the adjoining pigsties and dung heaps was indescribable. Epidemics of typhoid, typhus and cholera reduced the life expectancy of a mill operative living in these conditions to 18; a horrifying statistic!

It was not just the unfortunate mill workers who felt the effects of this urban transformation. Once pleasant areas of Preston were becoming surrounded by inferior housing, threatening the lifestyle of the better-off. They could move away if necessary, but, within the town, very little land was being used for good quality homes; it was presumably more lucrative to build cheap accommodation for rent. The need for more superior houses was just as acute. The cotton industry had generated great wealth and swelled the ranks of the middle classes; shop-keepers, solicitors, doctors and mill-owners were all looking for suitable homes for their families. This was the situation in Preston in the 1840s when an idea to build outside the town's boundaries was first considered.

Garstang Road looking north towards Withy Trees. On the right is the entrance to Victoria Road. The first two properties on the left have been demolished and replaced with a row of shops and a block of flats at the corner of Queens Road.

Fulwood Park

The move was made possible by the formation of a freehold land society in Preston. These societies multiplied as a result of the

Larch House was one the earliest Victorian properties to be built in Fulwood. It stood at the corner of Lytham Road and Garstang Road on land which is now occupied by the health centre. Its first occupant Abraham Sedgwick, a staunch Methodist who also owned some weavers' cottages at Windy Nook.

Reform Act of 1832, which extended the right to vote to persons who held a 'forty shilling freehold'. This meant that an individual who owned a property valued at forty shillings or more would qualify for a vote. In some areas this considerably increased the number of voters and was used to change the balance of power in county elections. As the political scene changed, land societies became simply a cheap means of providing building plots in the suburbs of our towns and cities.

In January 1850, a meeting was held to explain the objectives of the society. The *Preston Guardian*, owned by Joseph Livesey, the town's most ardent social reformer, recorded that these were 'to enable the industrious classes generally to have a voice in the election of the county representatives, and show them how, by their own exertions, aided by frugality and prudence, they can attain the dignity of freeholders.

Sharing the platform with 'frugality and prudence' was 'temperance', and at the following meeting, James Taylor, a travelling preacher of the teetotal movement, spoke for two hours on the benefits of these virtues. Whilst the aim of the society was to encourage working-class membership, the officials were all members of Preston's middle class. Among the founders of the group were John Goodair, a mill owner, who was elected president, and Joseph Livesey.

In practice, the society bought large areas of land and divided them into small plots which were then offered to members, who had bought shares through weekly instalments. The purchase of a suitable site was a priority for the society officials. When Fulwood Moor was enclosed in 1817 Samuel Horrocks, the mill owner, purchased forty-five acres of farmland on the north side of Eaves Brook, just within the township of Fulwood. In 1850, following the death of Mr Horrocks, the land was put up for sale and the trustees decided that this was perfect for their new housing estate. The sum of £4,995 was agreed upon and the estate conveyed to William Livesey and Michael Satterthwaite, as representatives

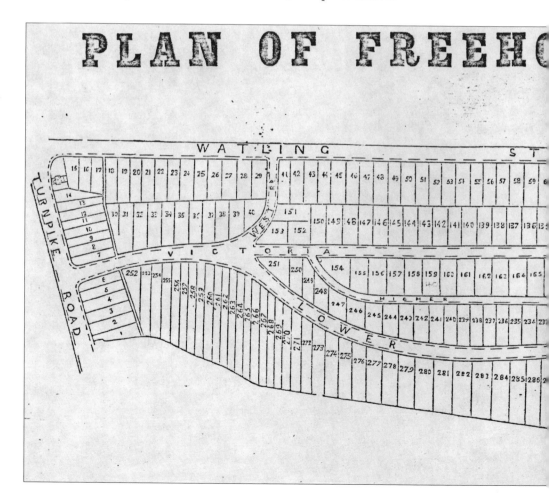

of the Preston Freehold Land Society. These names appear in the deeds of all the houses on the estate.

A Preston firm of architects and surveyors, called Myers and Veevers, were employed to design the layout of the estate. They took full advantage of the south-facing hillside which gave them scope to plan the roads in a gentle curve following the lie of the land. When the plans were complete, an advertisement was placed in the local paper and there was a huge response. Demand for the plots was oversubscribed, so allocation was determined by ballot. On 29 January 1851 one hundred and eighty-three shareholders gathered in the Temperance Hall in Preston. Their names were placed in a ballot box and drawing commenced for the 335 plots, which were sold for an average price of £30. Eight plots

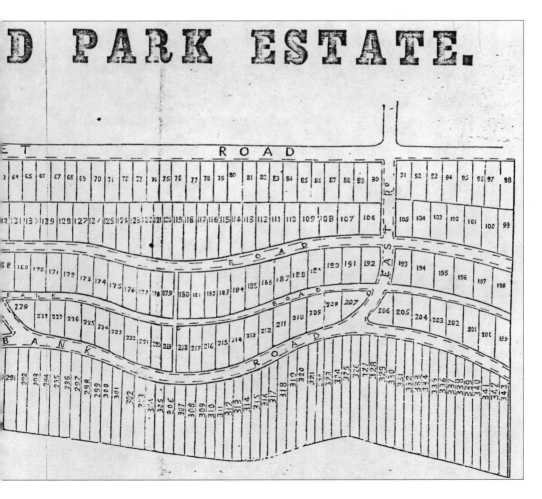

were retained by the society to provide income to pay the Church Tithe charges. These were on Garstang Road between Watling Street Road and Victoria Road – the site of Park Terrace.

Initial interest shown in the Freehold Park was encouraging. It was hoped that members would retain their plots and not resell for the sake of a quick profit but, inevitably, adverts were soon appearing in the columns of the *Preston Guardian*, placed by members tempted by a quick return on their investment. Those who retained their plots eagerly awaited further developments. The time had come for an official launch of this pioneering project and reporters from the *Preston Guardian* were on hand to record the event:

3rd May 1851 Freehold Park.

On Thursday last were laid the foundation stones of the first two houses of the Freehold Park. It being the opening day of the Great Exhibition, the parties intending to erect them (William Livesey and Robert Charnley) availed themselves of a day which could not fail to be remembered.

There was some little ceremony in connection with the affair, which is rather unusual at the commencement of private

Victoria Road *c.* 1900. The local children have come out to pose for the photographer at the junction of Victoria Road and Lower Bank Road. This was the main thoroughfare of the Freehold Park estate, and the route of the early horse drawn trams. The tramlines are just visible in the road.

Fayre Haven, featured on BBC television in 1996, was one of the last properties to be built on the Freehold estate in 1900. Its flamboyant architectural style was a complete contrast to its earlier Victorian neighbours and must have raised a few eyebrows whilst under construction.

dwellings. Under each foundation stone was placed a bottle, hermetically sealed, containing ground plans of the estate and rules, reports and various other documents relating to the rise and progress of the Preston Freehold Land Society.

Antony Hewitson in his book *Northward* recorded that the ceremony was preceded by a race between Livesey and Charnley, who were both eager to have the honour of laying the first stone. Mr Livesey was the winner, setting his stone down on the south side of Victoria Road, near the entrance to Lower Bank Road. The plot remained vacant until the turn of the century when it was bought by a successful Preston shop owner called J. R. Hodgson. He designed and built the house called *Fayre Haven* in a grand

'Arts and Crafts' style, which in 1996 featured in an episode of *The House Detectives* on BBC Television. On investigation, the house revealed a wealth of stained glass and original wallpaper which had obviously come from Hodgson's own decorating emporium.

Mr Hodgson started out as a poor painter and decorator who made his fortune and eventually became Mayor of Preston; a classic 'rags-to-riches' story which delighted the producers and viewers when the programme was screened in March 1997.

The first house to be completed on Victoria Road, opposite the entrance to Higher Bank Road, was a double-fronted house built by Peter Watson for his brother. The house originally had bay windows on each side of an attractive porchway, which were replaced in the early twentieth century when it became a butcher's shop. One or two of the earliest properties still have sash windows with numerous small panes. When plate glass manufacturing started after 1851 the more familiar two-pane sashes came into use.

Building progressed slowly at first; only eleven properties were occupied by 1853 when the first directory listing for the Freehold was recorded.

Harrison Bros., butchers, on Victoria Road. The first house completed on the Freehold Estate. At the turn of the century it was converted to a butcher's shop and remained so until the 1980's . It was built of rubble stone from Longridge and later smooth rendered. The shop window replaced a bay similar to the one on the right.

Residents of Fulwood Park 1853 – from Oakey Directory.

Mary Baines – independent means
Paul Berry – Boot and shoe manufacturer
Robert Charnley – House agent
Richard Fairbourn – Wholesale grocer/tea dealer
Thomas Houghton – Printer
Thomas Monk – Independent means
John Parnaby
John Threlfall – Retired tea dealer
Henry Watson – Iron founder
Peter Watson – Iron founder
William Whittam – Wholesale brewer

A detailed study of the growth of the Freehold Park by Judith Boxall (1993) revealed that the majority of these early residents had moved from addresses in Preston. The vast majority were middle class; businessmen, shopkeepers and office workers who were keen to move away from their places of business to the privacy of a separate home. Extensive research also charted the growth in the following decades: forty households were recorded

William Whittam's house, Willow House.

in the census returns of 1861, 97 in 1871, 108 in 1881, and 140 in 1891. Several plots had been combined giving the owner room for a grand villa. Mr Charnley, for example, bought the first seven on the south side of Victoria Road for Charnley Villa, which was set in beautifully landscaped gardens. It was later demolished and replaced with four semi-detached houses.

The size and design of properties built on the 'Freehold' varied enormously; from small farm cottages to gracious detached villas. To ensure that a reasonable standard was maintained, the trustees set building regulations which had to be complied with. For example, all houses had to have a rateable value of not less than £80 *per annum* and be constructed of brick, stone, iron and glass, with a slate roof. Market gardening and keeping of livestock were permitted, but pigsties had to be enclosed by a wall six-feet high. These rules seem to suggest that a mix of farm small holdings and suburban villas was quite acceptable, and that the purpose

Constitutional Cottage, Victoria Road. One of the smaller cottage style properties of the Freehold Estate. The naming of this house has remained a mystery; one suggestion is that it commemorated the ending of the American Civil War. The Cotton Famine caused by the war had catastrophic consequences for mill towns such as Preston.

Numbers 11 and 13, Lower Bank Road, built around 1870. The principal entrance to these large semi-detached villas was on the side elevation opening into an impressive square hall.

of the estate was not solely to re-house the new middle class. It has certainly left a variety of Victorian house styles to ponder over.

Farming cottages were usually quite simple, with a modest single doorway and plain sash windows. (Sometimes there were no windows on the back elevation.) Also they were often positioned at the corner of the plot, leaving more garden area. Constitutional Cottage, opposite Fulwood Club on Victoria Road, is a good example. Market gardeners did exceptionally well on the south-facing slopes of the estate. Here again, if the site was to be used commercially the house was positioned leaving most of the land free for greenhouses and allotments. Several large greenhouses were constructed on plots near the top of Plum Pudding Hill (Park Walk). However, these small holdings were in the minority and the estate soon developed into a haven for the new middle classes. They often designed their own homes taking ideas from standard pattern books from which they could select decorative features to embellish the facade. The most famous of these catalogues was the *Encyclopaedia of Cottage, Farm*

and Villa Architecture and Furniture by John Loudon, published in 1833 which was used by builders for several decades.

Many properties on Lower Bank Road have three or four floors. The basement and attic floors were the domain of the servants. All the cooking and washing was done 'below stairs' and the entrance to these quarters was usually by a separate door. For example, numbers 11 and 13 have their principal entrance on the side. The road-side entrance used today once opened directly into the housekeeper's area, from where stairs led down into the basement. Houses of this size had at least two reception rooms on the ground floor, and their loation on the south side of the building provided beautiful sunny living areas for the family with fine views over Eaves Brook valley and Moor park. Family bedrooms were on the first floor. Children were normally segregated; all the girls would sleep in one room and all the boys in another.

Before 1870 most houses did not have a bathroom. Hot water for washing would be brought by the servants to the bedroom, which was equipped with a washstand and a chamber pot. Towards the end of the century systems for circulating water around the house were invented and bathrooms became an integral part of the house. With the invention of piped water came the flushing

Thorneycroft, Higher Bank Road. This photograph is taken from Lower Bank Road. The soldier is standing at the front door which was approached by a winding path through the garden. Today, for convenience, these houses have their principle entrance on Higher Bank Road, but the road still retains its back-street charm and has several fine examples of Victorian coach houses.

toilet, which must have seemed the height of luxury after the outside privy.

Higher Bank Road was once the back road to properties on the north side of Lower Bank Road. Careful inspection of the south elevation of these houses will usually reveal the redundant front doorway which in many cases has now been altered to a french window. The long, sloping front garden may have looked impressive to the Victorian caller but does not lend itself to modern living. Now, all the houses have their principal entrances on Higher Bank Road. The odd coachhouse or old wash-house are reminders of the road's 'back street' heritage which somehow just adds to its charm.

Richard Veevers

Each house on the estate has a story to tell but, one in particular, is worthy of a special mention, for it was the home of one of Fulwood's most notable residents – Richard Veevers. The construction of his splendid villa on Lower Bank Road in 1859 must have caused quite a stir. *Woningworth* was no ordinary house,

Woningworth, seen from Blackpool Road. (*Reproduced by kind permission of the Harris Museum and Art Gallery*)

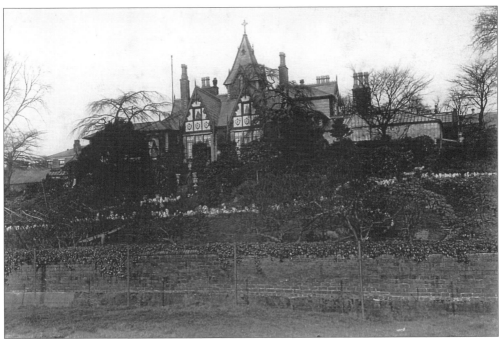

Woningworth. *c.* 1950. This splendid Victorian Gothic villa was the home of Richard Veevers, who was known as the 'managing director' of the Freehold Park. The grounds were originally hidden behind a castellated wall with turrets at each end. This was removed when the modern houses were built in the grounds. There is reputedly a tunnel leading from the house, underneath the road, to the coachhouse situated on Higher Bank Road.

One of the original gothic stone windows of Woningworth, with a beautifully decorated stained-glass panel.

This painting of Richard Veevers hung in Fulwood Council Offices until its closure in 1974 in recognition of his twenty-five years of service on the council. Under his guidance the council undertook several major construction schemes, such as the laying of the water mains.

its Gothic spire and elaborate leaded windows gave it an imposing appearance which far outshone its relatively modest neighbours. Mr Veevers was an architect and he became involved in the Freehold Park project at an early stage when his firm was commissioned to do the site's road plan. He entered into the development of the estate with great enthusiasm, and for the rest of his life worked wholeheartedly in forwarding the interests of Fulwood. His dedication was rewarded in 1863 when he was invited to chair the newly formed Local Board of Health, a position he held for twenty-five years. Under his guidance, many public service schemes were brought to fruition including water supply and sewerage construction. Richard and his wife Elizabeth Grace lived at Woningworth for forty years, until he moved to the Lake District shortly before his death in 1902. He is buried in Broughton Churchyard.

A bus service to Fulwood Park

As most of Fulwood's residents worked in Preston, public transport was urgently needed and Richard Veevers was quick to spot this business opportunity. In May 1859, he started the first horse bus service between Preston and Fulwood. After three months the enterprise changed hands and a year later, a new company was formed which ran this route for ten years and also ran a bus to Broughton. For twenty years, the little horse bus provided this essential service, but then the population grew sufficiently to attract the attention of the Preston Tramway Company. A scheme to lay tram tracks out to Fulwood was approved and work commenced in 1879. This tramway was worked by six cars and

The horse tram service started in 1879 and ran from Preston via Garstang Road, Victoria Road, East Road and Watling St Road to Fulwood barracks.

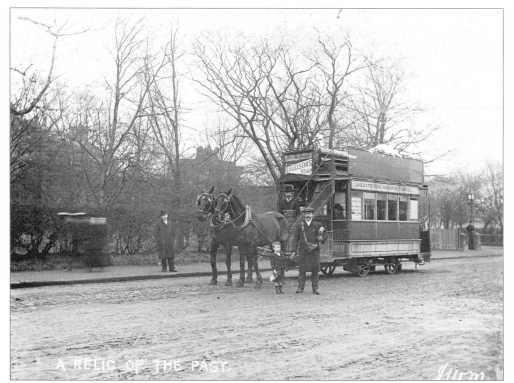

A RELIC OF THE PAST

An old tram shed which stood on Watling Street Road, just to the west of the Garrison Hotel. It was demolished and replaced with a terrace of three houses.

The electric trams ran via Watling Street Road rather than Victoria Road. The absence of any other traffic makes this scene almost unreognis-able, but the houses on the left have changed little.

twenty-five horses and operated to Fulwood Barracks via Victoria Road.

The turn of the century witnessed yet another change for commuters to Fulwood when horse power was replaced by electricity. The opportunity was taken to modify the well-established route to form a circuit which completed its journey back to Preston via Deepdale Road. The electric trams started their

135

journey in Lancaster Road near Miller Arcade and ran to Fulwood Barracks via Garstang Road and Watling Street Road. This route also made history on 15 December 1935 when the last ever tram to run in Preston made its farewell journey to Fulwood.

It was not just commuters who used the trams. For those who lived in the smoky confines of Preston, a trip on the tram to Fulwood was a rare treat, a brief respite from their own grim surroundings and a chance to look at the gracious homes of those who were fortunate enough to live there.

No. 2 Higher Bank Road. The name of the owner of this grocer's shop, J. Eyles, can be seen over the door. John and his wife Elizabeth ran the business from about 1890 until they retired, when their daughter, Martha took over. It was changed to a house after the Second World War. (*Photograph courtesy of Mr C.Shaw*)

Local shops and services

As the Fulwood community grew, retail and service traders established businesses in the area to serve local householders. There was a ready market for all kinds of foodstuffs and soon front rooms, usually in corner properties, were being converted into shops. There were once food retailers on the corner of Garstang Road, Higher Bank Road and the passageway opposite Fulwood

The Fulwood Café, which stood at the corner of Victoria Road and Garstang Road. It has now been replaced by a block of flats. (*Photograph courtesy of Mr D. Carwin*)

Club and on Watling Street Road. Small home-run businesses such as bakeries and laundries found regular custom in the neighbourhood. Farmers were on hand to provide fresh produce from the surrounding fields and newly-established market gardens. A great asset to the area was the sub-post office at the corner of Albert Road and Victoria Road, the first to be opened in the Preston district. At the rear of this building is a garage which started life as a coach house and, in the 1870s became a commercial livery stables run by George Wilkinson.

Sports and social clubs

Above Wilkinson's stables in Albert Road was a hayloft which some local young men decided to turn into a social club in the 1870s. The room, which was reached by a cat ladder, was decorated and furnished with easy chairs, a billiard table, and a chandelier. One of the founder members wrote in the *Northern Daily Telegraph* in 1929 of his fond memories of those days. He recalled how, after they had finished carrying up the furniture, he and his friends 'took a walk to Highgate Woods and there decided to have a contest to see who could jump furthest over the stream'. As evening fell the weary band returned home to face the consequences of desecrating the Sabbath and also of ruining their best suits into the bargain!

FULWOOD CLUB

Amongst the Trustees of Preston Freehold Land Society were several teetotallers who were adamant that there should be no beer-house on the estate. However, not all the residents were of the same mind and, no doubt, with a good measure of opposition, succeeded in founding Fulwood Club on Victoria Road. Records

Fulwood Club. *c.* 1900. Established in 1872, this Victorian men's club was a favourite venue for the first North End football team. Many a victory celebration has taken place around the bar. Here the members are gathered for President's Day; the one event in the year which ladies were allowed to attend. (*Photograph courtesy of Fulwood Club*)

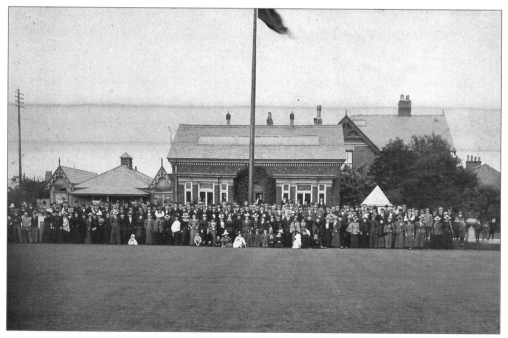

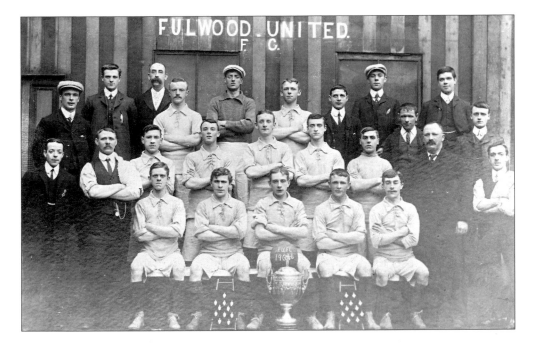

Fulwood United F.C. Fulwood had its own amateur football team who are seen here with an impressive collection of medals and a trophy won in the 1905–6 season.

can be traced back to 1872 when a plot of land was leased and a billiard hall and pavilion were duly erected. The club soon became a popular meeting place where a relaxing drink was certainly not frowned upon. Club accounts record the purchase of Whisky at £1 11s. 6d. per gallon, barrels of Beer at £4 5s. for thirty-six gallons, and wine and spirits at 21 shillings a gallon. Judging by the frequency of these purchases, the club was host to many a lively gathering in its early history.

Fulwood Club was closely associated with Preston North End in its formative years; Walter Pomfret, who played in North End's first team, was also a founder member of the bowling club. The team adopted the club as its 'watering hole' and it was possibly here that they made a decision to move to Deepdale. The close relationship between the two clubs lasted many years and Walter Pomfret was elected President of Fulwood Club when the lease was taken over by the members in 1894.

In 1900, the members formed a limited company and purchased the land and premises from the original owners. Through its long history, many annual events have featured in the club's calendar, the most important being President's Day when the men-only rule was relaxed and ladies were allowed over the threshold.

Perhaps one of the club's greatest days was in March 1887, when the North End team was carried shoulder high along Victoria Road after a triumphant cup match. The procession, led by a band playing 'See the conquering heroes come', turned into Fulwood Club where celebrations continued well into the night.

The clubhouse has been updated and extended several times but the club itself has changed little in its long history; bowls, snooker and companionship darts are enjoyed by members of this Victorian club to the present day.

FULWOOD TENNIS CLUB

In 1891 James Gregson agreed to rent a piece of his land at the corner of Highgate Avenue for the provision of three courts. The rent was a nominal sum and his generosity was certainly instrumental in the club's foundation. After six years, the membership had grown to 130 and the club re-opened on its present site with six courts, a croquet lawn and two pavilions. At the opening ceremony, the members congratulated themselves on the success of their institution which provided 'health giving recreation and pleasant social intercourse' for local residents.

PRESTON GOLF CLUB

One of Fulwood Park's residents, Nicholas Cockshutt, was a founder member of Preston Golf Club. In 1892, he and James Rigby, the Medical Officer of Health for Fulwood, decided that

Preston should have its own golf course and set about finding a suitable site. A nine-hole course was eventually sited on the north side of Brockholes Brow. It was nothing more than 'meadowland which had undergone a single week's preparation', but this did not deter would-be golfers. Within days the membership of Preston Golf Club numbered seventy. In 1894, a second club was formed in Fulwood which in its first year attracted nearly two hundred members. Many came from the surrounding area, but a surprising number travelled by tram from Preston, alighting at the workhouse and taking a short walk down Sharoe Green Lane. It was not long before the two clubs amalgamated, choosing Fulwood as their permanent home.

The land, rented from the Clayton Estate, was also farmed by tenant farmers who used it to graze their sheep and cattle. It was not an easy alliance. The animals were essential for keeping the grass short but they often strayed onto the greens, ruining the tireless efforts of a hardworking greenkeeper. For the first five years, a small pavilion served as the clubhouse but, as the membership grew, it became inadequate. By this time the Clayton family had sold the estate to the Rothwells. They were approached with a view to building a new clubhouse, and following these discussions, a suggestion was made that the club should rent the old Hall Farm house when the farmer's lease expired. This offer proved favourable and, in 1903, the golf club took over the ancient home of the Claytons. £650 was spent on improving the facilities; a bathroom being one major expense, the installation of electric lighting another. The approach road, now from Fulwood Hall Lane, was also repaired and the farmer agreed to move his pigs further away from it as 'they were unsightly and gave off a bad odour'.

The club had a surprisingly large number of lady members. In 1904 it was suggested that the number be 'limited to 90' following complaints that they were causing delays on the course. They were also restricted to a small room in the clubhouse where they could take tea.

During both World Wars the club offered the facilities of the course to the Commanding Officer at Fulwood Barracks. In 1939, this gesture was gratefully accepted and during the next five years the ground was used for training purposes. On the flatter part of the course trenches were dug and posts erected to prevent enemy planes landing. In 1943, a bombing range was created in a sandpit and golfing was suspended every Monday from 8. ooam to 6. oopm while live grenade throwing was in operation. By the end of the war the course was in poor condition; years of neglect, lack of finance, and military use had all taken their toll.

In 1950, the Rothwell Estate was put up for sale and the golf club given the option to purchase the course. The agreed price was £7,800 for all the land, the clubhouse and four acres of Mason's Wood. The change in ownership meant that the members could now plan their future at Fulwood secure in the knowledge that they were there to stay. Several alterations to the old building have since been made and now only the porch and great oak door recall its former existence as the manorial hall of Fulwood.

Rock Villa, 60 Higher bank Road. The builder of this house was a stone mason who was obviously exploiting his talents when he constructed his house entirely of stone. This photograph, taken in the garden of Rock Villa, records the wedding celebration of Ann Jane Hayhurst and James Smith in 1910. (*Photograph courtesy of Mrs D. Fraser*)

Rocklands, 67 Watling St Road. *c.* 1920. This grand Victorian villa was built around 1870 and was first occupied by Thomas Ord, a currier. The name may well have been inspired by an elaborate rockery built in the garden which incorporated a stone arch. Posing for the photographer are the family of Charles Webb, who owned the property from 1918 to 1962, after which the Abbeyfield Society converted it into retirement accommodation. A terrace of town houses was built on the site of this large garden in 1990. (*Reproduced with the kind permission of Mrs A. Iddon*)

Primrose Villa, Victoria Road *c.* 1900. Mr Joseph Livesey and family enjoying tea in the garden of Primrose Villa. In the background is one of several greenhouses which were erected on his land. These were demolished in 1912 when two houses on Park Walk were constructed. (*Photograph courtesy of Mr J. L. Coward*)

In the background is the 'Victory' built in the garden of Primrose Villa and fronting onto Chapman Road. The neighbours opposed the building because it was in front of the old building line. After its completion Mr Livesey named it the 'Victory', and, in protest, the enraged neighbours built a blank wall (which can be seen here) as high as the house. (*Photograph courtesy of Mr J. L. Coward*)

Fulwood Grammar School, on Victoria Road opposite Christ Church. The school was run by Samuel Bottrill from 1889 to the 1930s. It is now part of a sheltered housing complex; an extension has been added to this elevation.

Park Walk *c.* 1906. This pathway from Lower Bank Road to Moor Park was originally named Plum Pudding Hill. It was a favourite promenade for the ladies of Fulwood Park and nannies taking their charges to the swings. Market gardening businesses, like those in the picture, thrived on the sunny southern slopes. Mr Manley, who owned the one on the left sold his produce from a shop in his house at the top.

A section of a late nineteenth-century Ordnance Survey map showing the built-up Fulwood Park.

145

CHAPTER TEN

Victorian development of Black Bull Lane

FTER GARSTANG ROAD was built in the 1820s, the Old Lancaster Turnpike Lane (now Black Bull Lane), relieved of all the passing traffic, became a quiet backwater, home to its small group of resident farmers and smallholders. There were not many houses at the bottom of the lane, just the old thatched charity school at the top of the brow and a farmhouse down past the brook.

At the top end on the western side were Broughton Cottage (built in 1830s), Whittles Cottages, Scotts Farm, and Ingol Head Farm. On the east side were several farms with extensive orchards – Crow Trees, Marstons, Dobsons and Dewhursts, some cottages and one or two small holdings.

Sharoe Brook, which crossed the lane to the north, and Eaves

Scott's Farm, Black Bull Lane, *c.* 1960. This old farmhouse was demolished in the 1960s when the Wimpey housing estate was built. 'Scotts Wood' road recalls the name. In the eighteenth and nineteenth centuries a footpath from the house led through the fields to Lightfoot Lane.

Thomas Hayhurst of Highfield (1833–1910), founder of the group of families which developed the community of Black Bull Lane. The following five photographs are of his children and grandchildren all of whom lived in Black Bull Lane and were kindly loaned by Joan Fuller, Ann Heppell and Pauline Noblet).

Brook behind Plungington House, formed Fulwood's boundaries with the parishes of Broughton and Preston respectively. Nothing changed until a farmhouse called 'Highfield' was built, facing the highway near to Duck lane.

In 1858 this farm with sixteen acres of land was purchased for Thomas Hayhurst and Mary Atherton, his young bride. Both of their families must have been very impressed with the area because within the next thirty years a large number of relatives followed the young couple and built, or rented, over a dozen homes nearby. By the end of the century they owned acres of land and had established a small community of extended family members.

The bridegroom was Thomas Hayhurst, born in Longridge in 1833 and living at Fulwood Hall Farm. His father Joash, a gentleman-farmer, leased Fulwood Hall Farm from the Clayton family. The bride, Mary, was the daughter of John Atherton a well-to-do iron founder of Preston.

The young couple were taken to their marriage at Preston Parish Church in two carriages and pairs. (An old receipt shows that these were hired from Hardings Carriers for £1 4s. 0d.) For the rest of their lives they reared cattle on their land, at Highfield and brought up a family of six children. In their retirement they

Highfield House c. 1885. Thomas and Mary Hayhurst (née Atherton) with their family, John, Walter and James, Elizabeth, Olive and Mary. A typical Victorian family-portrait, posed by the photographer outside their home. Olive (seated centre) married William Patterson, and lived at 'Fernbank' No. 20 Black Bull Lane. Elizabeth Ellen married Henry Bibby (saddler of Orchard St), and lived at Cadley Villas on the lane.

The modern Highfield House.

moved across the road to 'Beacon Dene', and both died in that house, Mary in 1909 and Thomas in 1910.

An interesting anecdote about 'Highfield' tells how a local boy had noticed a young maid employed by the family. Following local custom he opened the back door of the house and threw his cap into the kitchen ('setting his cap at her'), thus making his 'intentions' known to the young lady.

When old Cadley School closed in 1865 the Atherton family bought the land from the Trustees. The plot of over two acres reached from the top of the brow down to Savick Brook and included the sandpit by the brookside. At the top of the hill Mr Atherton enclosed a section containing four plots on which he built the detached villas which are now numbers 18 to 26 Black Bull Lane. He called the site 'Cadley Terrace' and the houses were named Edge Hill, Fernbank, West View (now Hillcrest) and Mount Pleasant. The last house was divided into a semi-detached house. Various members of the family, including John Atherton, lived on Cadley Terrace. Others of the extensive Hayhurst/

Atherton descendants and in-laws bought or leased the new 'Cadley Villas' near Boys Lane. They lived at Breeze-hill, No. 1 Ash Villas (now numbered 99), Braemar on the corner, Beacon Dene, and across the lane at Primrose Cottage and Withy Cottage.

Their families – Patterson, O'Kane and Hayhurst – were cattle farmers and dealers; the Athertons, Dewhursts and Whiteheads were in the iron-foundry business. They were instrumental in opening up Black Bull Lane as a residential area, although most of the in-fill houses were not built until well into the twentieth century. Many of their old houses still have the same stone gate-posts, and stand well back from the lane on the old build-

The Patterson family outside 'Fernbank', No. 20 Black bull Lane (now St Cuthbert's parish vicarage) c. 1895. William Patterson (1856–1920) married Olive Hayhurst of Highfield House, and had five daughters and two sons. William was a butcher and cattle-dealer in Marsh Lane and when times were hard in Preston opened a free soup kitchen to feed the poor. He was known locally as a 'character' who employed a West Indian coachman to drive him about. On one occasion he had to be rescued from his burning dressing room over the front door when he fell asleep whilst smoking. In his retirement the couple moved to 'Braemar' at the corner of Boys Lane (now a dental surgery).

The Henderson family outside No. 1 Ash Villas, now 99 Black Bull Lane. *c.* 1900. Wallace and Ellen are seated with their nine children. Wallace, who was orphaned as a child, had built up a successful wholesale confectionery business with a shop first in Plungington Road and later in Friargate. He delivered his baking to other shops in a horse and carriage which were stabled at the back of the house down a back lane. Ellen who was the daughter of the coachman at Oak House, Garstang Road died in childbirth a year or two after this photograph and the eldest daughter Annie brought up the family in her place (pictured far right). The Hendersons were linked to the Atherton/Hayhurst family by the marriage of granddaughter Winifred M. Henderson to Bill Heppell both near neighbours.

ing-line. Although the road surface had been gravelled since about 1850 the pavements do not seem to have been paved. In 1867 Fulwood Board ordered Mr Atherton 'to find drain tiles for draining the road in front of his land on Cadley Turnpike' which they 'would lay and form a cinder path thereon.'

In 1871 Elizabeth Sharples (née Atherton) was warned by Fulwood Overseers that she must pay up the rent which she owed for the sand-pit by the brook. The arrears dated back seven years, one year at 2*d.* and six at 4*d.* She was warned that the rent was being increased to half-a-crown per year and if she did not settle

Three Cadley sisters. Kathleen, Molly, and Mabel, three of the daughters of John and Mary Elizabeth O'Kane (nee Patterson) of No. 1 Mount Pleasant (24 Black Bull Lane). They had a younger sister, Joan, and 2 brothers, Jack and Michael.

her bill within one week they would take possession and terminate her lease. Ten years later her family were still being pursued for rent due.

One of this family, George Sharples, set up the first telephone exchange in Preston in 1881. For £12 he would install a Gower's Improved Telephone, although Bell's patent telephones and Crossleys patent carbon transmitters were also available. By the end of that year he had 78 subscribers listed on a single sheet directory, and each paid annual charges of £8 to £12. Every morning his clerk at the exchange called each number to check that their lines were working.

The Atherton/Hayhurst land was farmed until the 1930s when

Four generations, 1939. Olive Patterson, daughter of Thomas Hayhurst with her daughter Mary O'Kane, grand-daughter Kathleen Kealy, great grand-daughter Mary (of Drogheda, Eire),

it was sold for residential development and became the site of Kings Drive, Atherton Road/Regents Drive cul-de-sacs, Southgate, Eastgate and Westgate. The houses were built by William Holmes, who picked one for himself at the corner of Eastgate. The name Atherton Road disappeared in the 1960s when the two cul-de-sacs were linked up and named Regent Drive, but the name lives on in Atherton House on Kings Drive, built in 1932 for John O'Kane. At the outbreak of war John (Jack) moved to Ireland to organise the supply of beef to the British market. Throughout the war years of acute food shortage he toured Ireland buying and rearing cattle which were shipped through Drogheda to his own lairages at Birkenhead docks.

Atherton House School 1941–1946

In 1941 Atherton House was not being used. It is a detached house with a large garden which overlooks the Harris fields. At about that time John's sister, Joan O'Kane of *Mount Pleasant* Black Bull Lane, after boarding school and a year at Fribourg University in Switzerland, had returned home just at the time of the outbreak of the war with Germany. With her career plans all awry she spent a year teaching in a preparatory school at *Manor Farm* in Sharoe Green Lane. At the end of that year, realising the need for a school for the Catholic children of Fulwood, and encouraged by the clergy, she opened her own school in Atherton House. Although intended mainly for Catholics, children of other faiths were welcomed, some of them coming from families of men in the armed forces stationed locally. The staff – Elsa Inglis, a Froebel-trained teacher, Molly Noblett (née O'Kane), BA (English), and Betty Baines – taught the usual subjects, and elocution and dance were also on the curriculum. Pupils were taken to swim in the nearby Harris Orphanage School pool.

Atherton House School. The pupils of the school in Kings Drive taken during the 1939–45 war years.

Troy Laundry 1908. Tom Finney Ltd now occupy the old laundry premises situated near the railway line on Lytham Road. This postcard, showing several sign-written delivery wagons going about their business, was taken in the laundry's heyday at the turn of the century. The message on the postcard is written by the Scoutmaster of the YMCA in Preston, asking how many 1st Fulwood scouts would be attending a gathering later that week. (*Reproduced with the kind permission of Mr D. Carwin*)

Throughout the war years, under difficult conditions Atherton House provided a happy school environment for about 45 younger children in West Fulwood. When the war ended and Joan O'Kane was to marry and leave Preston she had to close her school, and Atherton House then reverted to private use. Soon afterwards the primary school built by the parishioners of St Anthony's took over the education of local Catholic children.

Joan O'Kane (now Mrs Fuller of Derbyshire) has happy memories of her childhood in Black Bull Lane in the 1920s and '30s. Her home at 24, Mount Pleasant (along with all others in the road bar one pair), enjoyed open views from the front as far as the railway line, and behind, back to Garstang Road. The fields in front were marshy, overgrown with rushes and dog-daisies, and at the back a favourite gathering spot was by a huge oak tree down towards Savick Brook (possibly one of the last ancient Oaks of Fulwood Forest). The Morphet children at Ingolhead had the use of a pony and trap, and Joan, her brother Michael and cousin Bill

1st Fulwood Boy Scouts 1912. A corrugated iron hut, located near the railway line in Cadley, was the meeting place of this popular and well-equipped scout troop.

Black Bull Lane 1937. The photographer is standing at the corner of Queens Drive on Black Bull Lane. The scene today would be quite different. On the right is the busy entrance to Fulwood Leisure Centre and Fulwood High School. (*Reproduced by kind permission of the Lancashire Evening Post*)

Heppell, would spend many happy hours with them riding about the local fields and lanes and playing in John O'Kane's barns, and by the railway track. There were two wooden buildings converted into shops, Routledges on the brow of the hill and Birchalls cabin near to Highfield House, and there the youngsters gathered and bought their sweets and Mrs Birchall's delicious home made

155

LYTHAM ROAD, FULWOOD.

ice-cream. (Their parents would patronise the K'Dai, a more refined sweet shop opposite the Plungington Hotel.) In autumn, apples were a special treat from the orchards up the lane.

Those were halcyon days, when children could safely cycle off for picnics by the ponds and brooksides, and wander through the meadows. Joan and her friends were known to all in the small local community, and now in her retirement she recalls the past with great pleasure.

Nooklands

Nooklands is a small, attractive estate of Victorian villas situated on the west side of Garstang Road, just north of The Withy Trees. When the site was laid out in the late 1870s, the private road was lined with horse chestnut trees. One hundred years on, they now hide all but the roofs of these elegant nineteenth century homes.

The land on which the estate was built was previously owned by John Atherton and Thomas Hayhurst of Highfield House and had been part of Nook Farm, situated on the south side of Savick Brook, near the Windy Nook garage. In 1876, the Nook Land Co. Ltd was formed with the intention of purchasing the farmland and dividing it into building plots. One of the house builders was James Redman Bradshaw, who had a slating business in St Pauls Road and lived for a time at Ashgrove in Nooklands.

Lytham Road *c.* 1925. Viewed from the railway bridge, looking west towards Woodplumpton Road. The Savick Brook can be seen winding its way across the fields of the Tomlinson estate where the sheep are grazing. The land to the right is thought to be where the first Saxon settlement in Fulwood was sited. Hidden amongst the trees is Millbank House, part of the old mill hamlet, which was demolished in the 1930s. (*Reproduced by kind permission of the Lancashire Evening Post*)

A small section of the 1895 Ordnance Survey map, showing Black Bull Lane. Nooklands can just be seen on the right-hand side. Note, too, the Harris Orphanage and the Plungington Hotel. Savick Brook flows from right to left, and there is a 'brick works' on its banks.

From the outset it was to be an exclusive development aimed at the wealthier end of the middle-class market. The plots were planned in the shape of a half circle; nine houses with frontages onto Garstang Road, and eight around the perimeter road. Imposing cast-iron gates were erected at each end of the crescent which were reputedly manned by a keeper who also looked after the roadway. (They were removed during the Second World War.) The houses were built in the early 1880s and in January 1882 an advert appeared in the *Preston Herald* for villa residences in Nooklands to be let or sold; rents from £45 to £65.

The properties are all semi-detached, apart from one in the middle of the front block; however, the design of the houses does vary. Some are one room wide and quite long front to back. They have a basement floor to accommodate the kitchen, scullery, butler's pantry and washroom; two or three reception rooms on the ground floor; family bedrooms on the first floor and servants' quarters in the attic.

Two pairs of houses in the south-west corner are double fronted. Here again, the kitchen was situated in the basement but was connected to a service room above by a dumb waiter. In households of this size, it was usual to have two live-in servants. They worked very long hours but presumably found it preferable to toiling in one of Preston's cotton mills.

Each house was given a name and early directory listings confirm that Nooklands was one of the most fashionable addresses of the period; cotton manufacturers, solicitors, high-ranking military officers, engineers and merchants took up residence in the crescent.

In 1882, three residents on Garstang Road sat on Preston Council: William Bryham Roper at Burrowbank, who also became mayor in 1900; Joseph Foster, at Milburn House, who followed his father into their successful ironfounding business; and James Brown, a lard and oil merchant, who lived at Mayfield. The Chief Constable, Major Little, chose *Woodville* at the entrance to the crescent for his home. All these houses would have had a pleasant outlook across to Oak House and Highgate Park estates, and apart from the odd coach and horses very little traffic would have disturbed the peace of their surroundings.

CHAPTER ELEVEN

Local administration in Fulwood

RIOR to any suburban development in Fulwood, the district was governed by the Parish Vestry which consisted mainly of local landowners. The new middle class residents had very little say in how their township was run. This situation changed with the passing of the Public Health Act in 1848 which allowed districts to set up their own board of health, run at a local level. They were primarily authorised to make decisions on health issues but often their powers extended to law and order, building regulations and general management.

In 1863 Fulwood Local Board of Health was formed and an inaugural meeting was held at the Royal Garrision Hotel to elect officers. The chair was taken by James Naylor, but his term of office was short; he was succeeded by Richard Veevers the following year. James Stephenson was appointed clerk, and James Bibby was appointed surveyor.

The committee dealt with a whole range of issues; some trivial, but others of paramount importance to the welfare of the community. One of the first tasks was to set the rates. A general rate of two pence in the pound and a highway rate of one shilling in the pound were decided on for the first year.

Residents regularly reported their grievances on the state of the roads, footpaths and hedges; problems which the surveyor was directed to attend to. Even incidents of public nuisance were brought before the board. For example, in 1873, they resolved the case of Mrs Stephenson's son, Edward, who had been seen damaging the street lights. He was formally told that unless he repaired the damage done to the street lamps in question and apologised

Laying water mains in Fulwood.

Fulwood Council Offices *c.* 1900. Completed in 1877, the offices were built on the site of a toll keeper's house. The affairs of the township were run from here until 1974, when all urban district councils ceased to exist and Fulwood, reluctantly, became part of Preston Borough.

to the Board for his actions, a summons would be taken out against him.

Management decisions often brought the Board into conflict with Preston Town Council. The provision of their own water supply proved particularly difficult. Preston had originally

159

The headquarters of
Fulwood Fire Service!

Fulwood Steamer.
Described here as the
Fulwood Prize Fire
Brigade. The firemen are
posing with their
cherished Fulwood
Steamer which is kept at
the Lancashire
headquarters in
Broughton and can be
seen at the annual open
day.

supplied the township but their costs had risen to an unacceptable
level. This was resolved by the opening of the Fulwood works at
Whittingham in 1883.

Eaves Brook, the ancient boundary between the districts, also
caused numerous arguments about who was responsible for its
pollution.

Fulwood Police Station 1896. Standing outside their police home on Watling St Road are Police Sergeant Peter Smith (not in uniform), his wife Jessie and two of their six boys. When he retired in 1905, Sergeant Smith went to live in Glendale Terrace on Sharoe Green Lane. His pension was £68 18s. 10d. per year. After the building of the workhouse in 1868, local residents felt unsafe and requested a local police station. (*Reproduced with the kind permission of Mrs M. Proctor*)

Meetings of the Local Board took place at the Garrison Hotel for ten years, then in 1874 plans were approved for a purpose-built office on the site of the old toll house on Garstang Road, near The Withy Trees. Fulwood Council Office was completed in 1877 at a cost of £824 14s. 6d. Fulwood Fire service was run from a small stone building at the rear of the premises (now demolished). Their 'pride and joy' was the Fulwood Steamer, a steam-operated fire engine which was pulled to the scene of a fire by horse.

Crime in the township was not a big problem, but residents felt increasingly anxious about their safety after the opening of the workhouse in 1865. When the tramp house opened in 1868, this made matters worse, and shortly after a police station was built in Watling Street Road. The premises comprised a house for the police sergeant, offices and a court room where offenders were tried by a visiting magistrate.

The workhouse did cause a fair amount of work for the police sergeant who was regularly called out after inmates had absconded. On one occasion it was reported that they had taken to tearing up their workhouse clothes, no doubt as a protest.

Farmers called on the police when livestock was stolen from their field, and in cases of diseases such as anthrax, the police took charge of isolation procedures.

Local householders were usually law-abiding, though the odd case of drinking after hours or the antics of high-spirited young-sters were occasionally recorded in the log book. It was, however, a wealthy neighbourhood and cases of petty theft from the homes did occur from time to time.

Fulwood Local Board of Health was superseded in 1895 by Ful-wood Urban District Council. It had served the community for thirty-two years; twenty-five of those were under the chairmanship

Service to mark the closure of Fulwood Urban District Council 1974. Councillor Lawrence Cartwright leads the procession into Christ Church for a service to commemorate the work of Fulwood UDC. The Local Government Act 1972 reorganised the administration of local areas bringing to an end Fulwood's independence. The Council Offices on Garstang Road were sold and, since 1974, the township has been part of Preston Borough. The ornate board listing the chairmen of the Urban District Council since 1895 now hangs in Fulwood branch library. (*Reproduced by kind permission of Mr and Mrs N. Cartwright*)

The procession makes its way down Watling Street Road. (*Reproduced by kind permission of Mr and Mrs N. Cartwright*)

of Richard Veevers. Twice, in 1867 and 1879, the board fought off attempts by Preston Council to incorporate the township into the borough. In fact Fulwood remained self governing until 1974 when all urban district councils ceased to exist. This brought to an end nearly nine hundred years of cherished independence.

CHAPTER TWELVE

Places of worship

VICTORIAN housing estate would not have been complete without a church and the first to be built in the Fulwood area was Christ Church on Victoria Road.

Prior to any construction on the Freehold Park estate, a sale was held for the remaining buildings on the site of Horrocks Farm. The farmhouse which stood near the location of Christ Church was demolished, but the barn adjacent to it was purchased by a Methodist minister called Peter Watson who converted it to a house and chapel. Little is known about Brunswick Chapel

Christ Church. *c.* 1865. A group of parishioners has come out to pose for the photographer standing in Albert Road. To the right of the steeple is the spire of Mr Veever's house on Lower Bank Road – a view obscured by other buildings today.

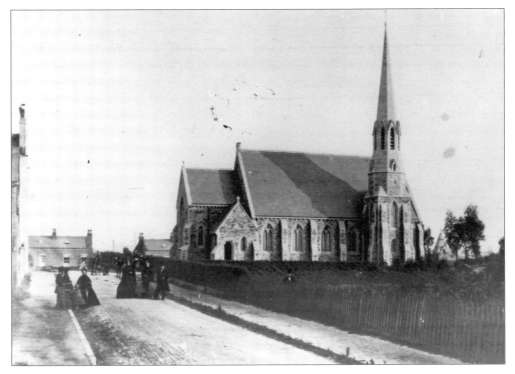

except that its closure was due to a serious disagreement between Peter Watson and his neighbours about his intention to develop the plot next to the chapel into a small workshop. The quarrel appears to have got out of hand and ultimately resulted in the minister being struck off the local preachers' plan, and the chapel being taken over by the Anglican church.

This seemed to be a popular change for the mission was well supported from the start. The first vicar, Reverend J. Woodhouse, launched an appeal to raise money to build a new church. The early 1860s were years of hardship for the people of Lancashire. The American Civil War had resulted in a shortage of raw cotton and many mills were forced to close, leaving workers with no source of income. The effects were felt at all levels of society because Preston's prosperity depended on the making of cotton cloth. Nevertheless, during these difficult years some major building projects were undertaken and one of these was the construction of Christ Church.

In two years £3,700 was raised, and a piece of land next to the mission was given by John Goodair. The foundation stone was laid on 19 May 1864 and the church, designed by Myres and Veevers, was completed the following year for a total cost of £5,000. Christ Church was consecrated in August 1865 and the first recorded baptism was the baby son of the vicar, Edward Joseph Hayes. The old mission continued to serve as a day school and all-purpose hall, where many impromptu concerts and fund-raising events were enjoyed by the local community.

St Cuthberts at Cadley

Historically, Fulwood was part of the parish of Lancaster but the opening of Christ Church lead to the creation of the new parish of Fulwood. As the population of the township grew the parish of Ribbleton was formed, followed in 1907 by the creation of St Cuthberts. For some time, a small congregation, under the guidance of Rev. A. Douglas, had been worshipping in St Cuthberts School in Plungington Road. The new church was built between 1914 and 1916 on land given by Sir William Tomlinson and consecrated on 25 July 1916. During its first 63 years it had only two vicars, the founder Rev. A. Douglas until he died in 1936,

St Cuthbert's, Lytham Road. The photographer probably climbed on to the railway bridge to snap St Cuthbert's Church. Opposite is the Troy Laundry and Carpet Beating Co., now Tom Finney Ltd.

Harvest Festival at St Cuthbert's Church. Many hours of work had gone into the decoration of church interior in readiness for Harvest Sunday.

and then his son-in-law. Rev. Alfred Morris who retired in 1970. The vicarage is in Black Bull Lane. The school is now closed and children attend Fulwood and Cadley School.

Fulwood Methodist Church

Methodism had grown steadily in Preston since the visits of John Wesley in the 1780s. The earliest meetings were held wherever his followers could gather, until the first chapel was built in Back Lane in 1787.

Lune Street Wesleyan Chapel followed in 1817, after which Methodist churches multiplied until most areas had their own.

In 1843, a purpose built meeting house called Cadley Wesleyan Schoolrooms opened in Fulwood. The chapel, which could seat sixty people, was run by Abraham Sedgwick who lived at Larch House opposite The Withy Trees. After a few years the number of worshippers appeared to dwindle and the Religious Census of 1851 recorded that a typical congregation was only fifteen. By 1860 the chapel had closed.

Brunswick Chapel on Victoria Road also had a short existence due to the discredited behaviour of its preacher Peter Watson. After its closure residents of Fulwood attended Moor Park Chapel

Fulwood Methodist Church. This view of Withy Trees taken from Lytham Road shows the newly built Methodist Church, completed in 1912. Now one of the busiest junctions in Fulwood; it is hard to imagine it was ever so tranquil.

167

on Garstang Road or small house gatherings, but it was felt that Fulwood should have its own chapel, so in 1896 the Fulwood Site Trustees formed to address the problem.

Their first task was to find a suitable plot and they were fortunate in acquiring land at the corner of Garstang Road and Watling Street Road from James Gregson of Highgate Park for

WESLEYAN CHURCH FULWOOD OPENING SERVICE BY REV. F.L. WISEMAN. B.A. PRESIDENT OF THE CONFERENCE

Following the opening service at the Methodist Church, a group of parishioners gather with Rev. Wiseman to record the event.

£855 5s. 11d. Fred Howarth was appointed architect and his plans for a cruciform church were approved, and building commenced. It was the fulfilment of a dream for Fulwood Methodists so they celebrated with two stone-laying ceremonies. The second raised £2622 19s. through members paying for the privilege of laying a stone or brick, and this raised almost half of the estimated cost of the finished building. Fulwood Wesleyan Methodist Church was dedicated on 26 September 1912. Initially, the chapel was a branch of Moor Park and did not have its own minister until 1939, when Rev. A. E. Folley became its first Minister.

Through both wars, the Methodist Church played an active role in local affairs, offering its premises and fellowship to strangers in the area. Between 1914 and 1918, Fulwood Barracks billeted hundreds of soldiers, many of whom marched to the church to attend its services on Sundays. Sunday school buildings were added in 1928. During the Second World War the church rooms were used as a day school for pupils evacuated from London and Manchester. It was then also that the uniformed organisations started to help young people through the dark days of the war. Fulwood Methodist Church is a familiar landmark opposite The Withy Trees and its spacious rooms are well used to the present day by a variety of clubs and organisations. Like all old churches it has been modernised over the years, but the character and overall appearance has changed little and is enhanced by the small adjoining garden, originally intended as the site of the manse. The open space provides a welcome show of trees and flowers in a predominantly built-up area.

One particular resident of Fulwood is remembered as a shining light in the local Methodist community. A small book of remembrance published in 1922 recalls the life of Agnes Threlfall (1848–1921) who lived for most of her life at *Laurel Bank* on Higher Bank Road. She dedicated her life to running the Sunday school at Moor Park Chapel and caring for the sick and needy in the community. On her daily treks between home and Chapel, she was a familiar sight and is fondly remembered in this description taken from the text:

> a somewhat dark and sombre looking figure, with a staid, quiet, methodical walk. In winter, she would be clad in a black cashmere skirt, over which was a dark plush coat, and a warm looking fur around her neck. In summer, a black silk cape took the place of the coat, and a soft light wrap displaced the fur. A bag for ear-trumpet, and the inseparable umbrella, completed the picture.

United Reformed Church

This church stands at the corner of Symonds Road and Garstang Road and was formed after the amalgamation of Garstang Road Congregational Church with St Margaret's Presbyterian Church.

In 1894, ministers of Preston's Congregational movement decided to open a Sunday school in Moor Park Academy, Brackenbury Road. Soon after, a piece of land was purchased from W. E. M. Tomlinson and a church, school and caretaker's house were duly built. Within the memorial stone, laid on 23 September 1897, were placed a statement of the history of Congregationalism in Preston, copies of three local papers of the day and a few coins, including a Diamond Jubilee medal. The church held its opening meeting in May 1899, presided over by Rev. Thomas Dearlove, its first minister.

By 1960, the Congregational Church was considering ways of relieving the growing cost of running their premises. St Margaret's congregation, since 1878, had held meetings in a converted foundry in St Paul's Square, which had also become expensive to maintain. A union between the two churches on the Garstang Road site, was proposed as a way of securing their future. In 1968 an inaugural service marked the start of a 'joint scheme of work and worship' and the two congregations entered a period of gradual integration. In 1972 they walked together in the Free Church Procession for Preston Guild, and in the following year completed their union to become the United Reformed Church.

Fulwood's first Catholic chapel

There was no Catholic church in old Fulwood until about 1858, when a privately-owned chapel was opened to serve the Catholics of the township. Two brothers, Revs. John and Thomas Smith, in 1857 purchased Broughton Cottage on Black Bull Lane near the junction with Garstang Road. The house was divided into

St Mary's Cottage, Black Bull Lane, with its statue of St Mary above the window. A matching statue of St Michael on the adjoining cottage had to be removed when it became unsafe. From 1860 to 1882 St Michael's private chapel served as a Mass-house for Catholics in Fulwood.

St Michael's Cottage,
Black Bull Lane. The
Sanctuary and altar of the
nineteenth-century chapel
with the statue of St
Mary and the
stained-glass window,
one carefully preserved
by the present owners.

two parts, numbers 6 and 7, and relatives made their home in one half. There was a large drawing room in No. 7, which the new owners extended by building another room onto the end of the house. Double doors separated this extension from the drawing room, and it was made into the Sanctuary which could be closed off when not in use. The walls were panelled with pinewood and, an altar built, set on marble pillars from Durham Cathedral. Above, a beautiful stained glass rose window was installed. A typtrich dated 1594, which had hung over the altar in the ancient chapel of Stydd in Ribchester, a carved oak reredos from Salmesbury, and a stone piscina completed the furnishings. The chapel was dedicated to St Michael, and the presbytery/family house next door, to St Mary. Stone statues of the two saints were placed on the outside wall above the front windows and a cross on the roof. (The statue of St Mary is still there today.)

The two priest brothers came from the Smith family who lived at Wards Farm and Clock House in Salwick near Clifton, and in 1800 built St Mary's church at Lea Town. They were active members of a network of Catholic Recusant families in rural Lancashire who concealed chapels and schools within their homes. Their intention in building St Michael's chapel in Fulwood was to provide a Mass centre for Catholics who lived in the area extending from Preston to Barton. It could hold a congregation of up to 100 people.

St Michaels and St Marys were owned by the Smith brothers until Thomas died in 1882. Since 1884 the houses have been in private hands.

The Carmelite Monastery

The Carmelite Convent on St Vincent's Road, although it is home to an enclosed Order of Contemplative nuns, has always been very much part of the local community.

Behind the high walls the Sisters live their private lives dedicated to prayer for the work of the Church and peace in the world. They support themselves by working in their printing office and providing Altar-breads to churches. A little shop inside the front door is stocked with a range of beautifully-produced greeting cards.

The red-brick building in five acres of gardens with vegetables and fruit trees, was purpose-built in 1917 and provides, simply and austerely, for the Sisters' chosen lifestyle. Contact with the outside world, although restricted is maintained through their commercial and hidden apostolate work, and limited access to the media. The lay peoples' part of the chapel is used regularly by supporters and local Catholics. Carmel could be described as a spiritual oasis in the centre of the hustle and bustle of twentieth-century Fulwood.

The peaceful cloisters of the Carmelite Convent on St Vincent's Road described as a spiritual oasis in the centre of the hustle and bustle of twentieth-century Fulwood.

St Anthony of Padua

The parish of St Anthony of Padua was founded in 1943 by Canon Michael Geoghegan who opened a temporary church in July 1945 with a wooden hut for parish activities. Some of the parishioners provided voluntary labour and over the years extensions to the church, a parish hall and school and in 1954 a new three classroom school, were all built, aided by their efforts. The parish had to maintain the school at its own expense for five years, until the education authorities adopted it as a county primary school. The church, designed by Gilbert Scott was opened in November 1959.

Our Lady and St Edwards

Situated on Marlborough Drive and built in the Romanesque style, this church was opened in June 1954 by Bishop T. Flynn. In 1965 the parish school in Lightfoot Lane was built. In the early years a hut was used for services and parish activities. More recently a new parish centre has been built. The parish developed rapidly and was divided into two with the founding of the daughter church of St Clare in 1971 on Sharoe Green Lane. The first building was the school, where church services were held until a temporary church was built in 1972. In 1978–9 the present modern church and presbytery were erected. The parish supplies the Catholic ministers for the nearby hospital.

Recent additions to the list of churches in Fulwood are the North Preston Evangelical Church, established in 1987 by an independent Baptist group of Christians who were eager to bring the Gospel to Sherwood, and the Free Methodist Church on Lightfoot Lane. Members of the Evangelical Church and their friends built the modern single-storey brick building in the centre of the estate from their own contributions, without any fund-raising. The Muslim community has also recently opened a mosque on Watling Street Road in a converted Victorian building which had previously been the Fulwood Park Hotel.

CHAPTER THIRTEEN

Fulwood – A refuge for the poor and homeless

HE CONSEQUENCES of Preston's industrial development in terms of social deprivation became more
apparent as the nineteenth century progressed.
Ambitious projects to address some of the problems
resulted in several fine buildings being erected in Fulwood. Little
public money was available for such schemes, so often their
foundation was due entirely to the determined efforts of charities
and the benevolence of local people. Large sums of money were
raised to build the impressive institutions which, even today,
stand proudly in their suburban surroundings. Aware that their
siting might be a contentious issue, great care was executed in
their design and large plots of land were purchased so that each
building could be enclosed in its own landscaped grounds. In
the latter half of the century, construction of five such establishments transformed the Fulwood skyline, each opening its
doors to those who sought refuge. In general, these self-contained
communities managed to live in harmony with Fulwood's more
prosperous natives, undoubtedly due to the strict regime under
which each was run.

The Union Workhouse

The debate on how to relieve the plight of the poor in Preston
raged for years. Practical proposals to form a union, bringing
together all the established workhouses in the area under one
administration was not popular with social reformers of the time.
However, arguments in favour of this system, which would reduce
the drain on the ratepayers' purse, won through, and in 1837 the

Preston Poor Law Union was formed. This gave authority to the Board of Guardians to supervise the running of several pauper establishments up until 1864, when proposals to replace them with one large workhouse took effect.

It was inevitable that the choice of location on Watling Street Road would cause some controversy, but construction of this massive building went ahead, taking three years to complete. It was designed by Leigh Hall in the Italianate style, inspired by the Renaissance palaces of Italy, with rounded Romanesque arched windows and a cupola clock tower. During the opening ceremony in December 1868, the Victorians congratulated themselves on what they saw as 'a mark of the progress of society' – the horrors and indignities of poverty were now hidden behind an impressive facade. The new building dominated the local neighbourhood; its huge clock tower showing the poor of Preston the way to its doors.

Antony Hewitson summed up local feeling when he wrote:

In an architectural sense, the establishment greatly improves the district but the rose has its thorn – Fulwood workhouse is the rendezvous of paupers and the roads to it are frequently lined with vagrants. These individuals operate somewhat

Preston Union Workhouse. The clock tower of this huge building has dominated the skyline for over a century. The iron railings which once enclosed the grounds were removed in the Second World War. After its closure in 1979, the building became Lancashire Health Authority headquarters.

inimically upon the fashionable conceptions and delicate nerves of the Fulwoodians who are beginning to have 'gentle blood' in their veins and can't stand the aroma of an aggregation of paupers.

The interior had many modern features, such as steam-powered heating and water-closets, but these facilities only glossed over the harsh prison-like regime under which the institution was run. Separate day-rooms and dormitories were provided for the in-mates, with females occupying the left of the building and males restricted to the right. They even entered by separate doors so that after admittance husbands, wives and children rarely saw each other. The workhouse deterred all but the sick, old and young from seeking its hospitality. The theories of its advocates appeared to be working; the stigma of pauperism was to be avoided if at all possible.

Few able-bodied men sought refuge in the workhouse, but those who did were given manual work to earn their keep. Tasks such as stone breaking or work in the extensive grounds were laborious and intended to deter all but hopeless cases. The local police force was often called to round up inmates who absconded, which worried the local community intensely. Compulsory wear-ing of a uniform aided this task but also provoked acts of rebellion; protests usually resulted in the tearing up of workhouse attire.

Children were taught a trade in the hope that this would assist them in finding work outside. Tailoring, cobbling and baking were industries which readily utilised this cheap labour and finding positions for boys was not difficult. Girls, on the other hand, were prepared for a life in service by assisting the women in the domestic drudgery of workhouse life.

In 1871 an infectious hospital was built at the rear of the workhouse. This was necessary because epidemics such as small-pox were common. Women inmates were given the task of nursing the sick but very few patients recovered from their illness and isolation only marginally checked the spread of the disease. The Local Board of Health continually monitored the general health of the township, but deliberately excluded the workhouse in their mortality counts, which were reported separately. Death rates at the workhouse were high; for example, in 1874, a total of 280 paupers died, a quarter of the workhouse population, and yet it did not appear to have given rise to any enquiry.

Very rarely were the cases of individual inmates recorded in detail, even though their lives were part of the intricate society which constituted Victorian Preston. Occasionally, when someone of note died in the workhouse, a local journalist might consider it newsworthy and a report would appear in the obituaries. This one was published in the *Preston Guardian* on 5 October 1885:

From Banking to Beggary

A few days ago, Mr Nicholas Arrowsmith, a representative of one of Preston's oldest families died in the Fulwood workhouse at the age of 67. His father, Richard Arrowsmith was one of the principal tradesmen of the town, carrying on a business in the market place as a draper and importer of Irish linens. In 1825, he founded a banking business which sadly went bankrupt.

Nicholas Arrowsmith, the younger son of the founder of the bank, who never took an active part in its management, lost a large sum of money. Leaving Preston, he tried his luck at sheep farming in Australia, but all his speculations turned bad and he returned to Preston an utterly broken man and took refuge in the workhouse where he died as above stated after a fit of apoplexy.

Fulwood workhouse was built at a time when attitudes to poverty were already under review. Research showed that destitution was often due to insufficient wages or lack of work caused by circumstances beyond the individual's control. Towards the end of the century, the prospect of a return to relief in the form of payments was under discussion. Old age pensions had been considered since the 1880s but were not implemented until 1908, and even then, were only paid to the very poor. In 1928, the Poor Law Guardians ceased to exist and responsibility passed to the local council. The workhouse was renamed the Civic Hostel in 1948 when it was then taken over by the Public Assistance Committee under the new National Health Service. The old building was modernised and this helped to soften its harsh Victorian image.

The workhouse finally closed in 1979 and the last fifty residents were transferred to new accommodation in Meadowfield House, Fulwood. The building was taken over by the Lancashire Health Authority who converted it to offices, and more recently, by the University of Central Lancashire.

The extensive front lawn, which was once covered with trees and gravel walks designed to be used for 'airing' the aged and infirm, is now a pleasant open garden, giving the passerby an uninterrupted vista of this splendid Victorian building, which was once a last resort for so many of Preston's poor.

The Harris Orphanage

Edmund Robert Harris was a wealthy lawyer who made his fortune buying and selling railway stock during the growth of the railway network in England. He also became the sole surviving member of the Harris family and trustee of a valuable estate. This quiet retiring man lived as a semi-recluse but became one of Preston's best remembered benefactors. On his death in 1877 he left £300,000 for the construction of public buildings in

The Harris Orphanage. The frontage of the school and chapel have changed little in its long history. The school was taken over by Lancashire County Council in 1940 and opened to 'outside' children. After the closure of the orphanage, the trustees decided to sell the site, and in 1983, the school moved to new premises off Lightfoot Lane. The University bought the entire site and the old schoolrooms were converted to a conference centre.

Harris Orphanage, Fulwood, Preston.

HARRIS ORPHANAGE,
SOUTH SIDE (Girls)

The orphanage was a showpiece institution. The children lived in these spacious houses behind the school, in the care of a house mother and father. Today, they house students from the University.

memory of his family. A third of this sum was to be used to establish an orphanage for children in Preston.

The Harris Trustees purchased a fourteen-acre site called Crow Trees Farm which had frontage onto the main road through Fulwood. It was an ideal location, only two miles from the centre of Preston, in a healthy country environment. Here, the trustees planned to build the finest orphanage there had ever been. Several institutions were visited before a decision was made to adopt the cottage style of accommodation recommended by Dr Barnardo. The children would live in small homes under the care of a house parent but still have the benefits of their own school, hospital and church.

The Harris Orphanage opened in 1888 and Mr T. R. Jolly was engaged as governor, assisted by his wife as matron. They dedicated their lives to the running of the home and, on the death of Mr Jolly on 1929, the post of governor was filled by his son-in-law Henry Bassett-Jones; the Jollys' daughter had already assumed the post of matron when her mother died.

Children seeking admission had to live within eight miles of Preston Town Hall. As places were oversubscribed careful selection was made and the most deserving cases accepted. Those fortunate enough to be offered a place – for sometimes the alternative was the workhouse – received the best possible care up to the age of fifteen. They were then returned into the care of a relative or friend wherever possible.

When the Harris celebrated its centenary in 1988 a reunion of former residents was held. They all had fond memories of their childhood home and one of the oldest surviving children, Miss Andy Anderton, wrote the following account of her stay at the Harris from 1912 to 1922. Andy and her bother David arrived at the orphanage on the evening of 8 January 1912. It was snowing. The children with their grandfather had walked from Withy Trees where the tram had dropped them off and they said their goodbyes outside the governor's office.

My life at the Harris Orphanage

I would like to stress that we were living in very beautiful surroundings with every amenity for the age: electric light, wooden floors, bathrooms, washrooms etc. We were all well, warmly clad and received a good education in the hands of Miss Bertha Catterall. Uniforms were worn by everyone; boys and girls alike in Navy Blue.

There were six houses, three for girls and three for boys. In addition, there was a house on the girls side which was the sewing and knitting rooms. All the clothes for the girls were made here and jerseys and stockings were made on a circular knitting machine for the boys. Further away was another larger house which was the hospital. I was once there for three months with something contagious; confined to bed all day doing nothing but 'resting'. I was not even allowed to read. One of the boys came in each day to clean the fire grate and light the fire. David came one day but we were not allowed to speak to each other, but that lovely smile of his made my day.

On the boys' side of the estate, there was a tailor's shop and a barber's. The boys had their own playground surrounded by trees. In each of the boys' homes there was a married couple who had no children of their own, known as 'Mother' and 'Father'. The lady looked after the children and the man did jobs on the estate. There was a massive field at the back of the houses where hay and fodder were grown for the animals. The front of the field was kept short for the children to play in fine weather and we had a lovely duck pond. In the centre of the estate was the 'lawn', a very beautiful lawn mowed and rolled by the boys

Girls at play in the Harris Grounds.

until it was immaculate. No-one was allowed to play on it but it was used for special days such as Commemoration Day and gymnastic displays.

The boys were taught gardening under the supervision of Mr Dixon and since we were practically self-supporting, they learnt all about growing vegetables, market gardening and flower growing. Mr Tyson was the tailor and barber. In his tailor's shop, he would sit on a platform cross-legged with his work all around him. The barber's shop was next door; we were sent here once a month for a haircut. Boys and girls alike except the girls had a fringe.

We were not allowed to visit each others homes although we could be friends with other girls at school. There was no conversation between boys and girls apart from the odd word in passing. I do not remember ever having a chat with my brother David.

On Sunday, we went to church morning and evening. In the

Drill for the boys. Daily exercise was an important part of the curriculum.

morning, it was either Emmanuel or Broughton. We liked Broughton best for it was a good walk and country all the way. Everyone lined up outside school for inspection. We all had to be spick and span; shoes polished, socks pulled up and hair tidy. Then we numbered off; the Governor would say 'Even numbers one step forward' or 'Odd numbers' ditto. If we were not precise the first time then we were put back in line and started again.

The gates, which were usually closed, were opened and off we would march. Miss Catterall made sure the road was clear before we crossed towards Little Sisters of the Poor. There was little traffic on Garstang Road in those days; the odd pony and trap or car or bicycle. It was about two miles to Broughton Church with very few houses along the way. On the left hand side was the Black Bull Hotel at the corner of Black Bull Lane and further on 'Fosters Folly', a big mansion [now the Lancashire Fire and Rescue Service Headquarters] built by a man called Foster. Rev. Collinson always met us and holding out his hand would say 'Welcome children'.

Sunday afternoon, after the dishes had been cleared we were taken for walks in the country . Our most frequent walk was to

Withy Trees, up Watling Street Road, down Sharoe Green Lane and home down the side of St Vincent's Boys Home where the boys would be playing football as we passed by. There was no outlet by road of any kind between the orphanage and Withy Trees except Duck Lane. Neither were there any roads all the way to Broughton other than those I have mentioned. Indeed, I don't remember any 'modern' roads or buildings having been started before I left Preston at sixteen. After tea every Sunday we went to our own church. It was beautiful but not consecrated and the Governor explained to us that weddings and funerals could not be held there. The choir was made up of girls and boys of the orphanage. Miss Catterall was the choir mistress and the organist.

School life

When the school bell rang each morning, we lined up behind the school; boys at one end, girls at the other, in order of height. Miss Catterall carried out an inspection to make sure we were clean and tidy and then we marched into school. Clogs made a clatter on the wooden floors, so the rule was to 'walk quietly into the classroom'.

The infants classroom was facing the door from the Governor's house and here began our first taste of discipline. Any child not able to assimilate lessons in the time available was stood in a corner with a conical hat on marked DUNCE. For bad behaviour, we were told to stand in the corner, face to the wall, hands on heads.

On Monday morning, we learnt the Collect for the week by heart and, for the rest of the week, said it in unison daily, followed by a prayer. We then filed out to the Boys' playground for drill. We had a very busy curriculum, starting each day with arithmetic. I remember school as a very happy period. Miss Catterall was quite strict, very clever, extremely musical and made learning a pleasure.

Once a week we would be taken out into the country for a Botany lesson, sometimes along Lightfoot Lane, Sharoe Green Lane and Durton Lane and, occasionally, to Squire Anderton's Wood, as far as the Shrine. The woodland lanes were a wonderland. We covered many miles, always looking for something; one time it was Cuckoo Pint, another time it was Deadly Nightshade or Woody Nightshade, Hips and Haws, Foxgloves, Wild Violets, Meadowsweet or Dragonflies. No plucking flowers or berries; this was strictly forbidden.

Home life

Life in our home was quite a different story; it was work all the way. There were about sixteen children in each home and every one of us had work to do – even the tiniest child could dust or polish forms. It may be hard to believe but ALL the duties in the homes were carried out by the children – girls and boys alike. There was no outside help whatsoever. The day started at 5.30 a.m. when two girls got up to clean the long black grate in the kitchen and get the fire going, ready for the porridge pan and the kettle. No one could get even a drink until the fire was drawing. Firewood and coals were brought in the previous night and newspapers were used to make spills which made it burn longer. The other girls were all up by six o'clock and before we ate breakfast the whole house was cleaned and polished from top to bottom. Porridge was served in big blue and white bowls with milk, followed by a slice of bread with treacle or syrup. We were all washed and scrubbed clean before breakfast and, when we had eaten and washed the dishes, we were off to school. In the evening, we had to busy ourselves with darning, mending and knitting lace collars for our dresses. When these tasks were done, we could read until bedtime. I remember at night, kneeling on our beds to see the Carmelite Convent as it was being built and weaving all kinds of imaginary yarns about it.

At the age of fourteen, we left school and were assigned to a special duty until we were released to our relatives or friends at the age of fifteen. When we were due to leave, the girls were taken to Goobys in Church Street to have a costume made and fitted with a straw hat to match.

My grandfather and Uncle Charles died while we were in the Harris Orphanage, but our very dear grandmother lived for quite a few years. When she died at the age of 86, not only did we lose a Grandmother but a very dear and true friend.

Miss Andy Anderton.

Little Sisters of the Poor

In recent years, this home for the elderly has been renamed the Jeanne Jugan Residence after the foundress of the religious order responsible for setting up and running the hospices, but the nuns, who are often seen out and about, will always be known by their familiar title the 'Little Sisters'.

The foundation can trace its beginnings to the year 1839 and a small coastal town in Brittany called Saint-Servan. Here, lived Jeanne Jugan, a forty-seven-year-old, poor, working woman who was touched with sympathy for the ageing poor of her town. In a time when there was no relief for the destitute, the old and sick were left to beg in the streets and Jeanne decided to take a blind and semi-paralysed old woman into her own home to care for her. Soon, other needy people were asking for assistance and offers of help came from younger girls who sought a religious life in which they could also serve others. To support her growing family, Jeanne went out on the streets with a collecting bowl and, in so doing, set an example for generations of Little Sisters since, who saw their humble quests for help as part of their work. From this small act of charity grew an organised religious community, known at first as the Servants of the Poor. Homes opened in

Jeanne Jugan Residence, known to most as the Little Sisters of the Poor. This photograph was taken from St Vincent's Road. To the right is the original building called Springfield House, built around 1870 for Dr Naylor. It was later occupied by the Hawkins family, cotton spinners, who sold the premises to the charity.

other towns and, in 1851, the work spread across the channel to London, where a home was established in Hammersmith.

Thirty years later, five Little Sisters arrived in Preston from Liverpool. Local people made them welcome and supported their work by donating furniture and kitchen utensils for their new home in St Georges Terrace on Deepdale Road. As always, demand for a place in the home was overwhelming and soon larger premises had to be found. In 1882, the foundation purchased a residence on Garstang Road in Fulwood called Springfield House, which they extended in 1893 with the large brick building visible from the road.

A hundred years on and the work of this Catholic charitable order continues with the same dedication that had been shown by those early pioneers in France. The close relationship which was established with the local community is as strong as ever, and appreciation of their valuable service is shown by the huge attendance at fundraising events and by donations given to the Sisters who patiently stand in public places to collect for their cause.

Derby Home for the Blind

In Victorian England, blind people were left to beg on the streets for food and shelter. There was no legislation to protect those who could not support themselves and their welfare lay in the hands of a few sympathetic social reformers. The town of Preston was fortunate in having several such men, the most notable being Joseph Livesey, who is best remembered for his association with the temperance movement. He gave his encouragement and financial backing to John Catterall, who was particularly moved by the plight of blind people. He felt they would be able to learn simple crafts in order to support themselves and, in 1864, rented a cottage on North Road as a workshop where the blind could work making baskets to be sold on the market. After three years, a public meeting was called to propose the setting up of an 'Industrial Institute for the Blind' which would find employment for the able blind in the community. In 1868, premises in Derby Lane were opened and fourteen blind workers moved in. The charity was well supported and the workshop was able to move

The Home for the Blind. As well as the production of baskets and mats, a thriving knitwear business was run from a workshop behind the home. A shop in Lune St was one of the outlets for their products. Sales in the late fifty's averaged £37,000 per annum but imports eventually affected sales, and gradually the businesses had to close.

to bigger accommodation in Main Sprit Weind where a school was added. Mr T. R. Jolly was appointed secretary in 1875, a position he held for forty four years.

Towards the end of the century, proposals were made to open a purpose-built centre for the education and employment of blind residents in Preston. The site on Lytham Road was acquired and the foundation stone was laid on 30 September 1893 by the Countess of Derby. The home was completed in 1895 at a cost of £5,980 and formally opened by Lord Derby, who later became president of the institute.

The passing of the Blind Persons Act in 1920 effectively handed responsibility for the care of the blind to county councils and the old age pension was extended to blind people at the age of fifty, but these changes in no way diminished the importance of the institute's work. In 1925, the Fulwood workshops were extended and the following year, a hostel was opened to accommodate twenty-four blind resident trainees. As the years passed, the institute redirected its resources into social centres, but the Fulwood site continued its work in education and training.

In 1945, the Ministry of Education gaves its approval for the school to change its remit and to educate partially-sighted children, which meant that blind pupils were moved to other schools. This was the first school of its kind in England and visitors came even from overseas to see the excellent work being done. The home finally closed in 1987 when new government policy recommended that partially-sighted pupils should be educated in mainstream schools. It was not a popular decision with pupils who had benefited from the specialist training for which the school was renowned, but its closure was confirmed and the building was sold and is now used as offices.

St Vincent's Poor Law School

The last nineteenth century institution to open in Fulwood was the Poor Law School which stood next to the Little Sisters of the Poor on Garstang Road. It was an institution in the traditional grand style of the Victorians – massive red brick walls adorned with turrets and a tower.

Funds for the construction of this boys' orphanage were raised in all the Catholic parishes of the town, which held a week-long 'Bazaar' at the Public Hall in Preston in 1891, and raised over £7,000 by their efforts. The home, opened by the Catholic Bishop of Liverpool in 1896, was built to house up to three hundred destitute Roman Catholic children. They were cared for by the Sisters of Charity who believed that a boy's development depended on the way he was treated when young. They were particularly concerned for the welfare of children in the workhouse who spent their days mixing with adult paupers.

The boys aged between three and fourteen came from all over Lancashire. They were given an excellent education which included practical skills such as knitting, darning, sewing and making raffia baskets. Music was high on the agenda; the school's brass band became renowned in the area and was often seen leading processions at festival times.

Unlike the Harris Orphanage where children lived in small family sized units, St Vincent's boys were accommodated in large dormitories which slept up to forty boys. In the corner was a small cubicle for the Sister who looked after them. Orphanage clothes and clogs were provided for the children but they did not each have their own set. On Saturday night, bath time, a pile

St Vincentt's Poor Law
School.

of clean uniforms were brought out for the boys, so they were clean and smart for church on Sunday. Religious education was an important part of the curriculum; many hours were spent learning prayers and hymns.

Once a year the boys were treated to one week's holiday in Lytham. They were housed in a school hall and spent their carefree days boating and bathing at the seaside.

At the age of fourteen the boys moved from the orphanage to St Vincent's Working Boys' Hostel on Deepdale Road. From here the boys were found work, quite probably in one of the many cotton mills in the town.

Closure of St Vincent's orphanage in 1956 came as a result of changes to government policy concerning the care of orphans. Fostering was considered to be a much better option, so that the number of children in institutions such as this gradually reduced. The home became a day school until 1960 and was then demolished. A new Catholic High School, now called Corpus Christi, was built on the site.

DUCHY AVENUE, FULWOOD.

CHAPTER FOURTEEN

The dawn of a new century

Winifred House, Garrison Road. Garrison Road did not exist when this house was built in 1907. Winifred House was designed and built by the architect Arnold Ellison, who was also the publican at the Garrison Hotel. The house originally had a very large garden with a tennis court but, in the 1920s, a pair of semi-detached houses were built at the far right end of the plot and Garrison Road was then laid out. Mrs Ellison moved to one of the new houses after the death of her husband and Winifred house was sold to Mr Cromleholme, a director of Lion Breweries, who supplied ales to the Garrison Hotel.

Duchy Avenue c. 1920. The gardens and trees look fairly mature on this early photograph of Duchy Avenue. The houses and those on Manor Avenue, Allenby Avenue and the east side of Fulwood Hall Lane date from about 1910 and were built on land belonging to the Manor house, which was later demolished.

HE EDWARDIAN PERIOD (1901–1910) could perhaps be described as Fulwood's 'golden age'. Following fifty years of residential development, confined mainly to the Freehold Park, the suburb had earned a reputation for 'exclusiveness'. Anthony Hewitson, writing in 1900, commented that Fulwood was what an American would term 'quite a place', occupied by 'a comparatively numerous and well-to-do population'.

There was a growing demand for housing in the area; most of the plots on the Freehold park had been built upon and builders were looking for land elsewhere in the suburb. Good profits could be made by local landowners from the sale of fields along the perimeters of their estates, especially if they were bounded by a road. Examples of Edwardian properties can be seen on Watling Street Road, east of Park Walk; on Manor Avenue; and on the north side of Watling Street Road and Highgate Avenue, near The Withy Trees. The latter development followed the sale of a portion of the Highgate Park Estate owned by James Gregson. The late Victorian terrace of six houses numbers 168–178 Garstang Road and the laying out of Highgate Avenue were completed before the turn of the century, but house construction was confined mainly to the years 1905–1910. Single plots were conveyed from the Gregson estate to the purchaser for about £150. A number of conditions of sale were imposed to ensure that properties were of a required standard; houses had to be valued at not less than £550, be at least twenty feet in width and have no back houses. No building was to be used as a public dance room or for the sale of ale, beer, wine, or spiritous liquors. These regulations were enforced by the local council. All the houses on Highgate Avenue were designed by local architects, such as P. H. S. Shepperd and E. J. Andrew.

The new generation of Fulwoodians wanted houses which embodied 'the spirit of a new age'. Properties were spacious, light and airy, and tastefully but simply adorned in the style of the 'Arts and Crafts' movement. Known also as the 'Queen Anne revival', this movement was inspired by William Morris in the 1860s, who felt that the industrialism of the nineteenth century was destroying the fabric of society. In 1861 he founded a firm to produce furniture in the old English country style using traditional handicraft skills. His products were to have a profound effect on design in general, and inspired a generation of architects who revolutionised the English house.

Men like C. F. A. Voysey and R. Norman Shaw applied the new ideas of 'Sweetness and Light' to domestic architecture and examples of their work are now important additions of our architectural heritage. Features such as Dutch gables, small panes of glass in white painted wooden windows, balconies and tall chimneys, were beautifully combined in small cottage-style homes. Well into the twentieth century, architects were still influenced by the 'Arts and Crafts' movement and this is exemplified in suburban roads such as Highgate Avenue.

In size Edwardian houses still resembled their Victorian predecessors, but were quite different in design. A fundamental change was the absence of a cellar, which meant that the kitchen and scullery had to be accommodated on the ground floor. Revolutionary changes to the decoration of exterior walls, windows and doors transformed the façade and made the houses more modern in appearance, and more practical. Walls were constructed of red brick, sometimes relieved with roughcast areas. High gables were often adorned with Tudor-style mock beams – a feature which was to predominate in suburban architecture for many years after. Imposing panelled and glazed doors covered by an elaborate canopy or porch were designed to welcome and impress visitors. Four porches at the eastern end of Highgate Avenue are supported on wood-turned pillars, painted white; a regular feature of Edwardian exteriors. Casement windows replaced the Victorian sashes and were decorated with white

Highgate Avenue. Most of the houses on Highgate Avenue were built between 1905 and 1910, a revolutionary period in the development of domestic architecture. The design of this pair of semi-detached houses in Highgate Avenue was inspired by the work of C. F. A. Voysey. His unique style is exemplified with their roughcast painted walls and long low windows. The style of 'Art Nouveau' is captured in the design of the unusual gateposts.

glazing bars, leaded lights and stained glass panels decorated with Art Nouveau flower designs.

The occupants of these new-style homes were the sons of Preston's wealthy families who had inherited fortunes made by their forefathers during the prosperous years of the nineteenth century. They were proud of their respectability and eager to proclaim their 'good connections' to all. Heraldic crests were occasionally incorporated into the decorative plasterwork, suggesting that the family had noble ancestry. *Holly House* has a crest in the gable which depicts two dragons. The house was built in 1905 for Charles F. Wilding Esq., a cotton manufacturer, and the dragons represent the Wilding family crest. The plans of the house also revealed that it was to have the ultimate symbol of the 'new age': a car shed.

The largest house on the avenue was built in 1913 for Richard Tinniswood Easterby, who was the deputy treasurer of Lancashire County Council and a Justice of the Peace. In 1910 he was living

Hallcroft, Highgate Avenue. Built just before the start of the First World War, Hallcroft was designed for a privileged society life-style which the war brought to an end. Employing servants after the war became increasingly difficult and houses such as this expensive to maintain. The beamed gable, wooden balcony and tall chimney are all typical features of the 'Arts & Crafts' style of architecture.

at No. 37, just opposite where he planned to build his grand mansion, Hallcroft. The grounds originally occupied a large corner plot which extended from the avenue down to Highgate woods. The gardens were beautifully laid out and included a tennis court (a must for all grand houses of the period), a gardener's cottage, chauffeur's house, stables and a garage. The house was constructed to a very high standard; even the bricks were specially made, each one stamped with Easterby's initials.

No expense was spared in fitting out the interior either; three reception rooms were furnished with elegant fireplaces and beautifully decorated plastered ceilings. The servants' quarters were separated from the rest of the house by a leather-backed door leading from the large oak-panelled hallway. A passageway led to the kitchen, scullery, walk-in pantry and butler's pantry, where glasses and crockery were kept. The staff lived on the premises, and their bedrooms, on the two upper floors, were reached by a second staircase. A house of this size would certainly have needed a large staff to keep it clean and running efficiently, and the number of servants one had was, of course, an indication of the family's wealth and social standing. Hallcroft was perhaps the last of the grand suburban mansions to be built in Fulwood. Large houses such as this became too big for the average family, so many were split into smaller units and some unfortunately demolished. Luckily, Hallcroft has been well cared for since the

Easterby family left and it is an exceptional example of early twentieth-century suburban style.

The First World War brought lasting changes to the way people lived and worked. Women, especially, did not want to see a return to the old order. They had discovered more interesting and better paid jobs, such as office work, and no longer wanted to do domestic work.

Times were changing, women were fighting for equality, and one of the suffragettes who helped to bring these changes about lived for a time in Fulwood. Edith Rigby (1872–1948) led the struggle to improve the conditions for working women in the early years of this century. Her father, Doctor Alexander Clement Rayner, spent most of his medical career caring for the poorest residents of Preston in an area known as the Weavers' Warren. As a child, Edith witnessed the suffering of these people and was appalled by the 'injustices of life'. When she was in her teens the family moved to Fulwood and lived in a house at the corner of Victoria Road and Garstang Road (now a newsagent's shop). During this time Edith was being educated at Penrhos College in North Wales.

Edith's exceptional life was recorded by her niece, Phoebe Hesketh, in two entertaining books, *What Can The Matter Be?* and *My Aunt Edith*. In one she describes the antics of her mischievous younger brother Harold, who, from his attic window, delighted in 'spraying passengers on the top-decks of passing trams with water from the garden syringe', presumably as they were turning into Victoria Road.

Edith married Dr Charles Rigby in 1893, at the age of twenty-one, and took up residence in Winckley Square. She worked tirelessly to improve the conditions of working women in the town. In 1899 she founded a club for working girls where they could go for a social evening with tea and biscuits for twopence. She also arranged classes in English literature, history and personal hygiene. Despite all her good works as a prison visitor, reformer, Sunday School teacher and campaigner, she was frowned upon by her contemporaries. Her involvement in disruptive behaviour to publicise the cause of the suffragette movement resulted in seven prison sentences.

She is perhaps best remembered for her daring exploits: in

1913, she pelted an anti-suffragette politician with black-puddings; she burned down Sir William Lever's bungalow on Rivington Pike; and she tarred Lord Derby's statue in Miller Park. The womens' suffrage campaign was brought to an end by the onset of the First World War, during which women proved themselves worthy of recognition by their invaluable contribution to the work force while the men were away serving in the army.

The Great War 1914–1918

When war broke out in August 1914, the streets of Preston were filled with crowds of people. Men came from all over Lancashire to enlist at Fulwood Barracks and, having nowhere to stay, slept rough in outbuildings and even under hedges.

Those chaotic days of mobilization at Fulwood barracks are recorded in the following memoirs of Private Ned Roe of the East Lancashire Regiment:

> Arrived in Preston at 7.10 a.m. Breakfast a drink or two in the County Arms and after an absence of close on 9 years the Barracks gates are closed once more and bolted behind me.
>
> Parade at 9 a.m. at Mobilization Stores. Every reservist has a shelf all to himself with a card tacked on to the top portion of the shelf bearing his rank, number and name. Your kit and equipment are stored away on this shelf, the rifles are in racks, also numbered. There is no delay, you simply file through and get equipped.
>
> We make bundles of our civilian clothes, address them and hand them into stores for despatch to our home addresses; or if you wish you can sell them for a song to a civilian who has obtained the contract for buying clothes. One pint per man allowed at 12 noon. Everyone is in uniform once again and all had a stiff medical inspection at 2pm. There is no room in the barracks rooms and quite a number slept on the square. We might as well get used to sleeping out.
>
> 400 NCOs and men parade at 11 a.m. We are bound for Colchester to join the first the 1st Battalion (East Lancashire Regiment). The Corporation kindly placed the tram services at our disposal and the inhabitants of proud Preston gave us a

rousing send off. I never saw as many lasses dressed up in clogs and shawls before. Where did they all come from?

As the war years dragged on, the tragedies and hardships suffered by local people and organisations increased. At the Harris Orphanage, finances were severely stretched but the children made extra savings and raised money for the children of Preston soldiers who had gone to the front. Spare places were filled by children orphaned by the war and, as casualties rose, the orphanage recorded with pride the names of 127 old boys who had 'answered the call'. A war memorial was erected outside the school in memory of eighteen former pupils who lost their lives. It was unveiled on 18 October 1924 and paid for by old boys and girls of the Harris.

WATLING ST. RD., FULWOOD.

SHAROE GREEN LANE, BROUGHTON.

CHAPTER FIFTEEN

Suburbia – a new extended Fulwood

Sharoe Green corner. Opposite the police station on Watling St Road, these four shops; a bakers, newsagent, chemist and hairdresser, once served the local community, who depended on shops within walking distance of their home. When the tobacconists was closed, smokers could buy their cigarettes from a dispenser on the pavement outside.

Sharoe Green Lane. Taken at the Black Bull junction with Garstang Road, the building on the left was demolished and replaced by a branch of the Midland Bank. The lane was once a trackway leading to Broughton Tower and the hamlet of Sharoe Green. Early settlers in the forest took this route off the old northern highway to their cleared enclosures and simple cottages. As the photograph indicates, the northern part of Sharoe Green Lane was at this time part of Broughton, the boundary being the stream just south of Yewlands Avenue.

Between the Wars

The inter-war period saw a huge increase in the number of houses built in Fulwood. House building had virtually come to a stand still after the outbreak of war, delaying a long overdue programme of rebuilding. In Preston, new housing was needed to replace dilapidated Victorian terraces and to accommodate a growing population. Government incentives were introduced which encouraged the sale of farmland, and generous subsidies were offered towards the cost of building. Suddenly the countryside around towns such as Preston was being carved into housing estates and laid out in avenues, closes and cul-de-sacs. It was a new style of suburbia, for a new generation of home seekers who now chose to purchase their home with a mortgage rather than pay rent. Most houses were designed on the familiar semi-detached plan with a hall, lounge, dining room and kitchen on the ground floor, and three bedrooms and a bathroom upstairs. Subtle variations helped to add a touch of individuality; for example, exteriors could be decorated with timber-boarding, hung tiles or rough rendered. The front garden was one area in which the occupier could use his own imagination, and sometimes this stretched to decorative features like a small pond or rockery – not forgetting the garden gnome!

The population in Fulwood in 1921 was about 6,500, but within thirty years this number had doubled. The main road north to Garstang, cutting through the rural north of the township, was an ideal arterial route to new estates. In 1934 the northern boundary of Fulwood was extended from the brook just south of Sharoe

GARSTANG ROAD, BROUGHTON.

Green Lane to Lightfoot Lane. This increased the area of the district from 2116 to 3273 acres, giving tremendous scope for further development.

One of the first large sales of land was a farm on the north side of Sharoe Green Lane, east of Garstang Road. Originally part of the Broughton Tower estate, it had been sold to Kirkham Grammar School, and later purchased by Richard Moon for £4,700. (The farmhouse, situated on Sharoe Green Lane, was demolished when Booths shopping complex was built in the 1970s.) Development on the land was gradual, starting at the northern end near the boundary with Broughton. Some of the first houses to be built were a row of bungalows in Moorlands Avenue which were sold for around £475 in 1927 – quite expensive for a small property at the time. The rise in the popularity of the bungalow was due partly to the fact that it appealed to older people who could afford a little more for their homes; and secondly, the payment of government subsidies for bungalows as opposed to houses was more valuable to the builder. This particular row of bungalows on Moorlands Avenue would have been completely surrounded with fields for several years after construction, but by 1938 the situation had changed completely

Garstang Road c. 1940. Looking south from Lightfoot Lane. The houses on the right-hand side are not yet built, but, just visible is Beech House on the corner of Beech Drive. In 1934 this point became the northern boundary of Fulwood and residents who had previously lived in Broughton became Fulwoodians overnight.

with the construction of Highfield Drive, Parklands, Brooklands, Brookfield and Woodlands Drives. Plots with frontages onto Garstang Road were filled with individually-designed detached houses, lending a certain prestige to the rows of semi-detached houses at the rear.

South of Sharoe Green Lane similar development was underway on both sides of the main road, with the creation of Hawkhurst Avenue and the Royal drives, Methuen and Raleigh Road, Yewlands Drive and Avenue and Greystock Avenue. The first few houses at the western end of Cadley Causeway were also completed during this period.

Intensive development along the corridor of the A6 continued up until the start of the Second World War, when construction was again halted for the duration. In some cases roads were laid out and remained unfinished; but the foundations of a new Fulwood were in place, awaiting a return to peacetime.

Fulwood – On the Home Front

The Second World War was declared on 3 September 1939. It was accepted soberly with none of the patriotic hysteria which had surrounded the start of the Great War. Fulwood Barracks again played an important part in the conscription of troops, equipping and training them for the battles to come.

At home, the threat of air-raids by enemy planes galvanised the home front into action. Cautionary preparations for the possibility of raids had begun in 1938 with air-raid drills, the construction of bomb shelters and the issue of gas masks. After the official declaration of war by Neville Chamberlain, the 'blackout' began, white lines were painted on kerbs and lampposts to help motorists and pedestrians, and all street signs were removed to confuse any invading Germans. Local councils recruited volunteers from the community as air-raid wardens, ambulance drivers, first-aid helpers and fire fighters. Training exercises by these groups became a familiar sight, and in Fulwood they were recorded by a photographer. He was also on hand at several important events throughout the war. A valuable collection of wartime photographs taken in Fulwood is now in the keeping of Lancashire Record Office.

Staged incidents were part of the training programme for volunteers in World War Two. Here three sections of Fulwood AFS under chief officer F. Taylor, practise fire drill at Highgate Park Estate. (*The photographs on pp. 204–9 are taken from LRO, UDFu 14/3, reproduced by kind permission of Preston Borough Council*)

The fire service co-ordinated with other services in this exercise on Sharoe Green Lane in 1939, in which ten victims were injured after an air-raid. Boys from St Vincent's School volunteered to be the victims.

Withy Trees. 1941. Fulwood Council Offices at Withy Trees was an operation control centre during the war. Temporary walls were built to protect the windows which doubled as billboards for advertising posters. This one marks the start of Salvage Week, July 1941.

Fulwood Fire Station. Withy Trees service station replaced the old fire station at the corner of Lytham Road. Before its demolition it was the home of the 'green goddesses', which were last used during fire service strikes in the 1980s.

Kitchen waste collection. 1941–42. Fulwood UDC waste cart advertising for bones.

Collecting kitchen waste to feed livestock was encouraged by catchy jingles posted on wagons and walls.

'Dig for Victory' was one of the great wartime slogans, first launched in a broadcast of October 1939. Lawns and flower beds were turned into vegetable plots and people were encouraged to rear chickens, rabbits and even pigs in their gardens.

The WVS outside Sanders & Son, the cake shop at Withy Trees collecting household goods from local residents. The little boy is handing over two kettles to the WVS.

Salute the Soldier Week. This week was to encourage people to invest in National Savings. The amount raised each day was listed on the target board on the front of the Council Offices.

United Nations Day. 1942. The troops and local people gathered at Withy Trees to hear a speech made by the Chairman of Fulwood UDC.

A poignant story of a wartime tragedy has recently come to light. In June 1944 a Mustang fighter plane which was being test-flown from the American airbase at Warton (now British Aerospace) developed a structural fault over Preston. As it flew northwards the plane began to disintegrate. The undercarriage wheel broke away and fell to the ground in Mill Lane. As the plane fell into a nosedive, the pilot struggled valiantly to prevent it from crashing onto Cadley Primary School, and finally he crash landed in a field by Ingol Head Farm on Walker Lane. Sadly, the pilot, 24-year-old Burtie Orth, was trapped and died in his burning cockpit.

Due to wartime censorship of military events, details of the crash were known only to a few people. In recent years, however, a group of aviation enthusiasts has located and excavated the site of the crash and unearthed parts of the plane. Local newspapers have chronicled their success, with contributions from the daughter of the pilot, who lives in Blackpool.

At the edge of a city

In the last ten years a major building programme has been underway at the eastern end of Fulwood called Longsands. It is

FULWOOD COUNTY SECONDARY SCHOOL, LANCASHIRE.   22149

expected to be the final phase of a project, formulated by the Central New Town Corporation in the 1970s, to provide homes for the growing population of the North West.

Discussions started as far back as 1951 with plans for an over-spill area for up to 47,500 people from Manchester, centred on Preston and Wigan. Within the scheme the rural districts surrounding Preston, including Fulwood, were identified as re-ception areas for up to 37,000 people. In 1965, the Minister of Housing and Local Government announced the Government's intention to go ahead with plans for a 'New Town' development. Following lengthy discussions, the designated area was finally confirmed in 1970 – a total of 35,000 acres, stretching from just north of Fulwood to the southern edge of Chorley. The whole area was divided into five townships (Fulwood was included with Preston) and each township was subjected to an in-depth survey before plans for future developments were proposed. The sharp contrast between the average living standards in Preston and Fulwood were highlighted in the resulting report; poor areas of the town centre were still awaiting slum clearance, whereas in

Fulwood High School. In 1953 these school buildings were the height of modernity. The long, low, classroom blocks with flat roofs have large expanses of window, typical of many educational premises built in the post war period. There was a desperate need for more secondary schools following the raising of the school leaving age to fifteen. Set amidst fields which have since been taken for housing, it must have been a popular choice with students of the time.

Fulwood, houses were generally of a high standard and, it was noted, there was room for many more.

The population of Fulwood had already increased considerably; from 12,809 in 1951, to 16,016 in 1961 and 21,785 in 1971. More recent house building, confined mainly to the private sector, was in the north-western corner of the district around Conway Drive and Lansdown Hill.

Central New Town Corporation proposed a new loop road to serve the eastern part of the district. It would give access to an employment area in the vicinity of Midgery Lane and to several new housing estates in the Longsands Lane area. The road, named Eastway, cost £2.3 million and was opened in April 1984. The first factory to be built in the employment area was for CCA Stationery Ltd.

During the same period there was growing public interest in the protection of sites of historic or architectural interest. The passing of the Civil Amenities Act in 1967 required local authorities to identify areas of interest and to designate them as Conservation Areas. They were then empowered to adopt measures to 'maintain and enhance their character'. Two areas of special interest were designated in Fulwood. The first, in 1975, was the Watling Street Road neighbourhood, including the Victorian housing estate, Fulwood Park, Highgate Avenue and the workhouse, followed in 1984 by the designation of the Harris Childrens' Home. Their special status protects all the buildings from harmful redevelopment or demolition. Any proposed alteration has to be in keeping within the age of the building and approved by the Council. Trees are also protected by similar County Council controls. For a period in the 1970s and '80s grants were made available to property owners towards the cost of repairs. This encouraged people to buy and renovate homes in old Fulwood, revitalising an area which had become somewhat neglected.

In 1974 Kennington Road County Primary School made the news with the opening of a new space-age style classroom. The prototype bubble is made of fibreglass and special insulating plastic and was originally conceived as a cheap alternative to conventional buildings, but when the cost of oil went up it was no longer a commercially viable option. The classroom is certainly a talking point; a functional, super-modern structure alongside a traditional Edwardian school.

The aim of the New Town Corporation was not simply to provide homes and workplaces but to create a pleasant environment for its new inhabitants. Local beauty spots were to be preserved if possible, and made more accessible by the addition of footpaths and cycleways. Fulwood, for all that it is now built up, abounds with such areas. They are to be found hugging the banks of the streams which flow, sometimes forgotten, under the roads and across the fields. For centuries, these streams have predetermined the fortunes of Fulwood. To early settlers they were lifelines, providing water for their homes and power to their mill; to travellers they were obstacles which made the journey north a trial.

The mighty oaks of the forest have long since disappeared, but the streams meander on, through the valleys of Fulwood, small pockets of woodland and meadow in a busy modern suburb – remnants of the once great Royal Forest of Fulwood.

Fulwood and Cadley County Primary School. The children of Class 6, 1998, are dressed as if the year is 1939. They were about to act the parts of evacuees, supposedly leaving their homes and moving to Chipping village school to avoid the bombing and wartime dangers. They could equally well have been wearing Charity School clothing and looking back three hundred years to the founding of their own school in the thatched building further down the lane.

Further reading

The First Millennium
Baines T., *Lancs. & Cheshire Past & Present*, Div. I & II
Dobson W., 1862, *History of Preston Guild*
Hunt D., 1992, *History of Preston*
Jackson G., *Broughton Roundabout*
Hallam J., 1979, *The Surviving Past*
Cunliffe Shaw R., *The Royal Forest of Lancaster*
Dalton E. A., 1903, *History of Ireland*, vol. 1
Wood M., 1981, *In Search of the Dark Ages*
Wainwright F. T,. 1975, *Scandinavian England*
The Record Society of Lancs & Cheshire, vol. 125
Farrer, *Lancs Pipe Rolls and Early Charters*
Eddius Stephanus, *Life of St Wilfrid* (quoted by Rev. Gradwell of Claughton in
    'Palatine Notebook', April 1883.

The Formation of the Royal Forest of Fulwood
Cunliffe Shaw, R. *The Royal Forest of Lancaster*
Victoria History of Lancashire, vols II & VII
Lancashire Pipe Rolls No. 416
Baines, *History of Lancashire*, vol. II
Div II, *Ecclesiastical History*
LRO DDPd 6/2, Edict of King Charles 1630

Cadley – A clearing in the Forest
Record Society of Lancs and Cheshire, vols 49, 54 & 87
Lancaster Assizes Rolls
Victoria History of Lancashire, vol. VII
Chetham Society, vol. 144 (1901) & vol. 87
Catholic Record Society, vol. VI
Gregson M., *History & Antiquities of Lancashire*, 1817
Jackson. Rev G., *Broughton Roundabout*
Richardson J., *Local Historian's Encyclopaedia*, 1986

The Claytons of Fulwood Hall
Stewart-Brown R., *The Pedigree of the Claytons of Crooke, Fulwood and Adlington in
    the County of Lancaster*
Smith T. A., Parker K. R., *On Fulwood Green*
Fishwick P., 434 Hearth Tax Returns for Fulwood

The formation of Cadley Village
LRO DDPd 6/1, Pedder papers (Elizabethan Inquerry of 1599)

Cadley Mill
Escourt & Payne, *The English Catholic Non jurors of 1715*
Lancs and Cheshire Record Soc., vol. 98
Preston Court Leet Records
LRO, WRW wills: Oliver Hatch 1715; Jas Knowles 1819; George Knowles 1857

LRO, UDFu/2, Minute book of Fulwood Overseers of the Poor
LRO, DDPd 6/ – 6/1 Elizabethan Inquerry 1599

Cadley School
Hewitson A., *Northward*
Local Gleanings of Lancs. & Cheshire
Preston Guardian, 19 Nov. 1864, report of allotment of land
LRO, UDFu 25/4 Charity Commissioner's report, 1926
LRO, UDFu /2 Minute Book of Fulwood Overseers
LRO, AE1/4 Enclosure Award, 1817
LRO, DRB1/83 Tithe Map, 1847
LRO, PR1496 Lease of land at Whittingham, 1713
Preston Guardian, 19 Nov. 1864, unsigned letter

Manorial Fulwood
Church Register. St John's Preston.
Berry. A. J., *Peter Walkden's diary*; *History of Preston*
LRO, QSP 1836/1, 1800/1 Overseers of the Poor report
LRO, PR 2020, 2021, 2022
LRO, Towneley Transcripts MF 1/4 Probate of wills & MF 1/34
LRO, WRWA/1720 & 1732

The recusant Catholics of Fulwood and Cadley
Blundell, F. O., *Old Catholic Lancashire*
Escourt and Payne, *The English Catholic Non juror*
Foley, Rev. B. C., *Martyrs of the Lancaster Diocese*
Victoria County History, vol. VII
Catholic Record Society, vol. VI (1909)

Sword, pestilence and famine
Lancs & Cheshire Record Soc, vol. 90
Church registers St John's, Preston; St Anne's Woodplumpton
Bull S., 1991, *The Civil War in Lancashire*
Chetham Society, vol. 72 (1864)

Passing through Fulwood
Thompson Watkin. W., *Roman Lancashire*
Hardwick. C., *History of Preston*
Garlick T., *Roman Lancashire*
Hallam J., *Archaeology in the Central Lancashire New Town*
Record Society of Lancs. & Cheshire, nos 125, 128
Baines E., *History of Lancs. and Cheshire*
LRO, DDPd25/34 Plan of Lancaster Canal

The Enclosure of Fulwood and Cadley Moors
Hodgkiss A. G., *A History of the County Palatine in Early Maps*
Fishwick, *History of Preston*
Commission for the New Towns Survey, 1980
Crosby A., 1991, *The History of Preston Guild*
LRO, DDPd 6/7 Letter suggesting difficulties in enclosing the moor
LRO, DDX 103/12 & 13 Enclosure Award. 1817

The King's 96 Acres
Preston Guardian, 20 Nov 1847
Fairfax J., *Northern Turf History*
Lummis W. M., 1978, *George Smith of Rorke's Drift*
Fulwood Barracks Museum Pageants & Parades, June 1998.
Authentic Records of the Guild Merchant of Preston, 1822.
LRO, DDX 103/4, Minutes of Fulwood Racecourse
LRO, DDK 29/3, Lease of Manors of Cadley & Fulwood 1806
LRO, DDK 809/2, Plan of Racecourse.
LRO, DDK 809/1, Lease in Fulwood viz Racecourse, 1813

A Home in the Suburbs
The Country Houses of Fulwood
Preston Guardian, obituary, F. Hollins, 9 Nov. 1907
Brochure of sale 1924 Greyfriars
Lancashire Evening Post, 25 Oct. 1960, Sale of Oak House
Gregson J., 1985, Personal recollections, Will-James Gregson
Preston Guardian, obituary: J. Gregson, 25 Dec. 1906
LRO, DDX 398–114, Letter, 1844, E. Grimshaw
LRO, DDX 595/9, Cadley bank Estate Plan
Census returns 1861/1871/1881

Fulwood Park
Dyos H. J., 1977, *Victorian Suburb*
Barrett H./Phillips J., 1987, *Suburban Style*
Boxall J., 1993, *Suburbanisation – A study of Fulwood Park*
Preston Guardian 3 May 1851; 17 May 1851; 31 May 1851
LRO, DDPr 37/104 Rules of Freehold Land Society
LRO, DDPr 141/11 Plan of Freehold Park
LRO, UDFu Minutes of Local Board of Health
Lancashire Daily Post, obituary: Richard Veevers, 24 Feb. 1902
Tramway Review, vol. 9, no. 67 'The tramways of Preston', G. Heywood

Sports & Social Clubs
Northern Daily Telegraph 1929 (Harris Reference Library Local cuttings)
Minutes of Fulwood Club
Smith T. A. Parker K. R., *On Fulwood Green*

Churches and Chapels
Hewitson A., *Churches and Chapels*
Porter H., 1987, *History of Fulwood Methodist Church*
Pitcher M., 1998, *Fulwood United Reformed Church*
LRO, Dp 441, Statement of Peter Watson, 1855
Flintoff T. R., *Preston Churches and Chapels*

A home for the poor and needy
Hewiton A., *Churches and Chapels*
Torr J., *The Poor of Preston and the New Union Workhouse*
Preston Guardian, 5th Oct. 1885, Banking to Beggary.
Anderton Miss A., *My Life at the Harris Orphanage*
Little Sisters of the Poor, Centenary Booklet, 1981
Institute of Blind Welfare ,100 years booklet, 1967
Lancashire Evening Post, 9 Nov. 1995, 'St Vincents'
Lancashire Catholic Voice Memories – Jim Martin

Towards the millennium
Street Directories of Preston
Lancashire Evening Post, 11 Oct. 1956, obituary, R. T. Easterby
LRO, UDFu 26, Plans submitted to FUDC
Hesketh P., 1985, *What Can the Matter Be?*

The Home Front
LRO, UDFu 14/3, FUDC Photograph album

Suburbia – A new extended Fulwood
Central Lancashire Development Corporation, Outline Plan, 1974.
Pearce G., Hems L., Hennessy B., *Conservation Areas in N.W. England*

List of Subscibers

Missing numbers in the sequence indicate where subscribers requested anonymity.

1　Tom and Anne Costich, Fulwood
2　Felicity Jane Barton, Fulwood
3　Brian Lowe, Fulwood
4　Anne B. Yates, Fulwood
5　Mr A. G. Moss, Fulwood
6　Mrs Anne Walmsley, Fulwood
7　William Higginson, Fulwood
8　Mrs Audrey Iddon, Fulwood
9　Brian B. Kirkham, Fulwood
10　Mr Anthony Hugh Swift, Fulwood
11　Tony Barker, Fulwood
12　A. Napoleon, Fulwood
13　Dorothy and John Roberts, Fulwood
14　Mrs Ena Battersby, Fulwood
15　Bill Higginson, Fulwood
16　Mr D. E. Cunnington, Fulwood
19　Mr and Mrs S. Morey, Fulwood
20　John and Pam Allen, Fulwood
21　John Siddall and Mavis Siddall, Fulwood
22　M. N. and R. E. Seed, Fulwood
23　Mr Charles Lewis Milton, Fulwood
24　J. M. Moody, Fulwood
25　Mrs Christine Vickers; Greg Vickers, Fulwood
26　L. P. McGinty, Ashton
27　J. T. and K. M. Sutton, Fulwood
28　Alan R. W. Jones, Fulwood
29　Hayley Louise Joan Smith, Fulwood
30　Mr Peter Latus, Fulwood
31　Margaret and Richard Lodge, Fulwood
32　Ron Severs, Fulwood
33　Alan Topping, Fulwood
34　Edwin Worth, Fulwood
35　Miss Margaret Powell, Fulwood
36　Gerard Johnson, Whernside Manor
37　Mrs Ann Porter, Fulwood
39　Ian L. Coward, Fulwood
40　Mr D. E. Killender, Fulwood
41　Monica Wilkinson, Fulwood
42　The Odd Chair Company, Fulwood
43　C. J. Spencer, Fulwood

44　Mr and Mrs D. I. Winstanley, Fulwood
45　(Mrs) Brenda R. Rainford, Fulwood
47　Jack Kilshaw, Fulwood
48　Mrs H. Jopling, Fulwood
49　W. K. Hutton, Fulwood
50　Mrs M. C. Addison, Fulwood
51　Pauline and David Walker, Fulwood
53　Mrs Susan Victoria Egan, Fulwood
54　Mrs Joan Kitchen, Fulwood
55　J. P. Corking, Fulwood
56　Meriel Nutter, Fulwood
58　Mrs Mary Pye, Fulwood
60　K. J. Moody, Fulwood
61　Mr A. Pearson, Fulwood
63　Mr E. Winders, Fulwood
64　Mr Ian Burgess, Fulwood
65　Michael Turner, Fulwood
66　Alban and Jayne Lakeland, Fulwood
67　Margaret Mackenzie, Fulwood
68　Mr and Mrs John F. Bury, Fulwood
69　Mr and Mrs S. H. McTaggart, Fulwood
71　Mr Fredrick. E. Midghall, Fulwood
72　Malcolm Anderton, Fulwood
73　Mr E. R. Hayes, Fulwood
74　Elaine Berry, Fulwood
75　William. N. Borrow, Fulwood
76　Mr A. R. Jameson, Fulwood
77　Mrs Andrea Wilson, Fulwood
78　A. Ogden, Fulwood
79　Anthony Peers Fothergill, Fulwood
80　Richard Bamford, Fulwood
81　J. Anthony Hodgson, Fulwood
82　Peter Sagar Aikman, Fulwood
83　Mrs Kathleen Riley, Fulwood
84　Carol Ann Rutter, Fulwood
85　Mr T. Deighton and Mrs M. P. Deighton, Fulwood
86　Gordon William Clarke, Fulwood
87　Mr A. B. Nightingale, Fulwood
88　Mr Brendan Hurley, Fulwood

89　Mr Eric F. Evans and Mrs Alicia M. Evans, Fulwood
90　Donald Ethell, Fulwood
91　Mr P. A. Turner, Fulwood
92　David E. Ridout, Fulwood
93　John Thompson, Fulwood
94　Mr C. R. Eastham, Fulwood
95　Mr and Mrs A. J. Clayton, Fulwood
96　Dr Frank W. Salter, Fulwood
97　Dr M. J. Trenouth, Fulwood
98　Derek Howarth, Fulwood
99　Mr Gerald and Mrs Ida Jordan, Fulwood
100　Mr A. and Mrs Y. J. Holland, Fulwood
101　Mr J. Threlfall, Fulwood
102　Michael Wright, Fulwood
103　Frank Gilman, Fulwood
104　Linda and Neil Carr, Fulwood
105　Alan Slater, Fulwood
107　Glenice Parker, Fulwood
108　Michael Hall Fletcher, Fulwood
109　Joseph Anthony Finch, Kieth
110　David Thomas Lamb, Fulwood
111　Mr and Mrs R. Funair, Fulwood
112　Mr P. Mullin, Fulwood
113　Mrs Patricia Jane Wedgewood Hussain, Fulwood
114　Arthur Saunders, Fulwood
115　Paul J. Eastham, Fulwood
116　John Wilkinson, Fulwood
117　Mr P. Cray, Fulwood
118　A. Wilson, Fulwood
119　Mrs Vera Marsden, Fulwood
120　Mr and Mrs R. Steel, Fulwood
122　Colin and June Foster, Fulwood
124　Mrs S. A. Brown, Fulwood
125　Richard J. Fiddler, Fulwood
126　David Kerry, Fulwood
127　Christopher Kerry, Fulwood
128　Eric and Doreen Welsby, Fulwood
129　Veronica and Ray Sanders, Fulwood
130　Joyce and Mike Hughes, Fulwood
132　Mr Peter Sullivan, Fulwood
133　Peter Cuerden, Fulwood
134　Mr B. Woodward, Fulwood

136 Alan Mather, Fulwood
137 Carolene and David Nash, Fulwood
138 Mrs R. M. Harrison, Fulwood
140 Mr William Wallace, Fulwood
143 Kenneth Heaton, Fulwood
144 Doreen Mann, Fulwood
145 Mr Eric Clayton, Fulwood
146 Collin Durnan, Fulwood
147 Miss B. Fielding, Fulwood
148 Edward T. White, Fulwood
149 Mr Mark Livesey, Fulwood
150 Mrs V. Leigh, Fulwood
151 Mrs Dorothy Hardacre, Fulwood
152 Lilian Robinson, Fulwood
153 Mr and Mrs A. C. Shufflebotham, Fulwood
154 Mrs Mary Proctor, Fulwood
156 Mrs Christine Wearden, Fulwood
157 Marie Oulton, Fulwood
159 Cyril Milton Ashcroft, Fulwood
160 Mr Richard Newsham, Fulwood
161 Mr Alan May, Fulwood
163 Gordon and Roxane Johnson, Fulwood
164 Beryl Ann Howard, Fulwood
165 Mr Thomas C. Smith, Fulwood
166 Mr and Mrs J. D. Carwin, Fulwood
167 M. W. and S. M. Jackson, Fulwood
168 Joanne Bury, Fulwood
170 Mrs M. Catherall, Fulwood
171 Mr D. A. and Mrs M. Booth, Fulwood
173 Lynne and Colin Harrison, Fulwood
174 Mrs B. Graham, Fulwood
175 Mrs E. Dunn, Fulwood
176 Mr Nathan Corless, Fulwood
177 Bernard and Marie Harrison, Pinner
178 Mr Thomas Owen Swinson, Fulwood
179 Mr and Mrs A. P. Collins, Fulwood
180 Mr and Mrs D. Worthington, Fulwood
181 S. Davis, Fulwood
182 Noel and Mary Hammond, Fulwood
183 Bernadette Purcer, Fulwood
184 Daniel and Matthew Garratt, Fulwood
185 Kenneth Chapman, Leyland
186 Mrs D. M. Cooley, Fulwood
188 Gavin Dashfield, Fulwood

190 Mr and Mrs T. L. Billington, Fulwood
191 Mrs Indrani Gurusinghe, Fulwood
192 The Royal Bank Of Scotland Plc, Fulwood
193 Mr Paul R. Finley, Fulwood
194 Dr J. L. Banik, Fulwood
195 Mr and Mrs K. W. Pickup, Fulwood
196 Robert McWilliam, Fulwood
197 Mrs Gabriella B. Maritan-Thomson, Fulwood
198 Miss Francesca D. Maritan, Fulwood
199 Michael F. Bathgate, Fulwood
200 Mr and Mrs June and Tony Johnston, Fulwood
201 Mr and Mrs S. H. Mounsey, Fulwood
202 Mr Robert Alan Driver, Fulwood
203 Mr and Mrs R. Chatburn, Fulwood
204 Mr S. C. Cavies, Fulwood
205 Margaret Turner and Peter Turner, Fulwood
206 Mr Pete Smith, Fulwood
207 Mrs M. M. O'Connor, Fulwood
208 Bill Shannon, Fulwood
209 John Glover, Fulwood
210 Lydia Jane Quine, Fulwood
211 Tony Roberts, Fulwood
212 Mr D. M. Collins, Fulwood
213 Stuart and Jayne Horrocks, Fulwood
214 Laurence, Linda, Rebecca, and Michael Gardner, Fulwood
215 Dr D. and Mrs K. Thursfield, Fulwood
217 John C. and Susan C. Law, Fulwood
218 John Peter Melling, Fulwood
219 J. B. and A. M. Frankland, Leyland
220 Howard, Andrea and David Casson, Fulwood
221 Mrs H. Young, Fulwood
222 Prof and Mrs R. W. and G. M. Hoyle, Fulwood
224 John and Mary Almond, Fulwood
225 Mr W. R. Smith, Fulwood
226 John and Judith Green, Fulwood
227 Chris Rawcliffe, Fulwood
228 Ged Carter, Fulwood
229 Mrs B. A. Ryan, Fulwood
230 Mrs Joan Osbourne, Fulwood
231 Mr J. T. Burscough, Lancaster

234 Stephen Bainbridge, Fulwood
235 Mrs L. Walsh, Farington Moss
236 Mrs M. S. Eastham, Fulwood
237 Mr and Mrs S. G. Eastham, Fulwood
238 Mrs R. Houston, Fulwood
239 Ian W. Shaw - Sue K. Landale, Fulwood
240 Mr and Mrs T. E. Willan, Fulwood
241 David G. Birkett and Halina Birkett, Fulwood
242 Valerie Hardaker, Fulwood
243 John Durnian, Fulwood
244 Marian Roberts, Fulwood
245 Mr and Mrs J. Cunliffe, Fulwood
246 Tom and Michaela McDonnell, Fulwood
247 Richard Jones, Fulwood
248 Mr J. F. and Mrs F. M. Burrow, Fulwood
249 J. A. Cowperthwaite, Leicester
250 Walter William Halsall, Fulwood
251 David John Porter, Fulwood
252 Marjorie Drake, Fulwood
253 Mr Eric Short, Grimsargh
254 Mr and Mrs D. Holdsworth, Fulwood
255 Teresa F. M. Harrison, Fulwood
256 W. S. Marsden, Broughton
258 Ian and Elaine Clement, Fulwood
259 Mr and Mrs P. Pacey, Fulwood
260 Mr and Mrs J. Milton, Fulwood
261 Mr R. and Mrs G. J. Sunderland, Fulwood
263 Mrs M. B. Elliott, Fulwood
265 Mr and Mrs S. C. Horsfield, Fulwood
267 Mrs Frances Isherwood, Fulwood
268 Hilary Quigg, Fulwood
269 Mr Vincent and Mrs Elizabeth Smalley, Longsands
270 Carol and Steve Rawlinson, Fulwood
272 Mr C. G. Keighley, Fulwood
273 Mr and Mrs Ken and Barbara Fisher, Fulwood
275 Joseph Fleming, Fulwood
276 Lucy Burscough, Fulwood
278 David Preston, Fulwood
279 R. L. Smith, Fulwood
280 Mrs A. W. Thompson, Fulwood
281 Mr and Mrs R. Roters, Penwortham
282 Paul and Anne-Marie Rotheram, Fulwood

284 Mr and Mrs K. Burns, Fulwood
285 Mr J. A. Bright, Lea
286 Caroline Hulme, Fulwood
287 D. A. Jackson, Preston
289 John and Karen Lucas, Fulwood
290 William Anthony Windle, Fulwood
291 Mr Barry Sowerby, Fulwood
292 Luke Garbutt and Finn Garbutt, County Down
294 Joan and Allan Jackson, Fulwood
295 Christopher R. Shaw, Fulwood
296 Aidan Turner-Bishop, Frenchwood
297 Mr and Mrs J. Parkinson, Fulwood
298 J. Andrew T. Patten, Fulwood
299 George Lambert, Fulwood
300 Mrs Suzanne and Mr Peter Bruce Macalpine, Fulwood
302 Dr Clifford J. Garratt, Fulwood
303 Gill and Graham Bath, Fulwood
304 Richard Peter Hardman, Fulwood
305 Helen Tomlinson, Fulwood
306 Mr F. and Mrs L. Welton, Fulwood
307 Chris and Jane Pink, Fulwood
308 Doug Greenwood, Fulwood
310 Mary Berry, Fulwood
311 John and Sunita Owen, Fulwood
312 Mr A. Summers, Fulwood
313 Mrs F. M. Fender, Fulwood
314 Ronald Westall, Fulwood
315 Mr D. Morton, Blackpool
316 Prof. J. D. Hepworth, Fulwood
317 Mr N. Cartwright, Fulwood
318 Mr J. E. Smith, Fulwood
319 Karl Zaldats, Fulwood
320 Diane Ogden and David Hegarty, Fulwood
322 Jacqueline Cousins, Fulwood
324 Mr Thomas Caine, Fulwood
325 Mr D. Cross, Fulwood
326 Mrs I. M. Hamilton, Fulwood
327 Michael Kirwan, Fulwood
328 Susan T. Bromley, Fulwood 12.10.1948
329 Mr S. Keighley, Fulwood
330 William Mayor, Fulwood
331 Andrew Gorton, Fulwood
332 Mr Martin Taylor, Fulwood
333 Jack Middleton, Fulwood
334 Ted Harrison, Leeds
335 Mrs Emily Ray, Fulwood
337 Mr R. Hester, Goosnargh
338 Catherine Latham, Fulwood
339 Joyce Rae, Fulwood

340 A. M. Dunsmore, Fulwood
341 Jill Sharples, Fulwood
342 Mrs Elizabeth Clack, Fulwood
343 Mrs E. S. Wild, Fulwood
344 Harold Fisher, Fulwood
345 R.W. and S. C. Dawson, Fulwood
346 Grace Parker, Fulwood
347 Alexander James Smith, Fulwood
348 June Chew, Fulwood
349 Master Daniel William Moon, Fulwood
350 Mr William Dainty, Fulwood
351 Mr Harold Cornall, Fulwood
352 Robin Howarth, Cottam
353 Sheila O'Gara, Fulwood
354 Alan Parkinson, Fulwood
355 Mr Raymond Francis Tapper, Fulwood
356 Mrs I. V. Barton, Fulwood
357 Stephen L. Pearce, Fulwood
358 John Michael Gallagher and Gwendolyn Humphreys, Fulwood
359 Dr G. W. Hurst, Fulwood
360 Richard David Thomson, Fulwood
361 Darren and Janet Cornall, Barton
362 Mrs E. J. Tonge, Fulwood
364 Geoffrey Woodhall, Fulwood
365 G. A. Pettit (Secretary Preston Historical Society), Fulwood
366 Mr and Mrs Harold Sutcliffe, Fulwood
367 Sandra Dixon, Whittle-le-Woods
368 Mr and Mrs M. T. Machin, Fulwood
369 Janet Hollinghurst, Fulwood
370 Susan Duckett, Fulwood
371 Mr P. B. Clement, Fulwood
372 Mrs B. Bryan, Fulwood
373 Mr S. J. Hayes, Fulwood
374 N. B. Atkinson, Fulwood
376 Gary D. Wood, Fulwood
377 Mrs Susan Walmsley, Fulwood
378 Mr Reg Smith, Fulwood
379 Michael Parker, Fulwood
380 Mrs Sheila Leach, Fulwood
381 Emma and Nicholas Burscough, Fulwood
382 Michael Swift, Fulwood
383 J. M. Smith, Fulwood
384 Mr James Brady, Ashton
385 Shirley Harris, Fulwood
386 H. G. Frudd, Fulwood
387 Mr and Mrs R. Greenwood, Fulwood

388 Mr Paul Edwards, Fulwood
390 Thomas E. Hamilton, Fulwood
391 Karen H. Williams, North Wales
392 Ken and Shirley Duggan, Fulwood
393 Mr H. E. Lees, Fulwood
394 Brian Chilton, Fulwood
395 Dr J. Eyre, Fulwood
396 Margaret and Peter Welton, Cottam
397 George Duck, Fulwood
398 Mavis Rogerson, Fulwood
400 Madeleine Hardy, Mossley
401 Simon Hardy, Mossley
402 Mrs E. Clegg, Fulwood
403 Miss D. L. Thompson, Fulwood
404 Mr J. Leeming, Ashton
405 Rex Walmsley, Fulwood
406 Paul McGuirk, Fulwood
407 Michael S. Archer, Fulwood
408 Andrew and Wendy Bennett, Fulwood
409 Jack and Carrol Turner, Fulwood
410 S. E. Robson, Fulwood
411 Mr and Mrs S. J. Hodgson, Fulwood
413 Mrs H. Wickham, Fulwood
414 Linda Coral Guise, Fulwood
415 Mrs Christina Rose Barton, Fulwood
418 Sharon, Kathryn, John and Mary O'Gara, Fulwood
419 Paul Ethrington, Fulwood
421 Mrs Joyce Muir, Fulwood
422 Mrs V. L. Peacock, Fulwood
423 Paul Mason, Lea
424 Mr and Mrs G. Dickinson, Fulwood
425 Alan John Pike, Ashton
426 Mrs Susan Wilson, Fulwood
427 Doreen and Tony Thorp, Fulwood
428 Pamela E. Thorp, Fulwood
429 Mrs M. C. Moulding, Fulwood
430 Ms Theresa Worrall and Neil Patterson, Fulwood
433 Keith and Patricia Sedgewick, Fulwood
434 Christopher Haworth, Fulwood
435 Lawrence Miller, Fulwood
436 Eric, Catherine, Sonya and Daniel Richardson, Fulwood
441 Bill and Pat Sumner, Fulwood
442 Nicky and Tony Goddard, Fulwood
443 Alan and Janet Rayner, Fulwood
444 Veronica Judge, Fulwood